Meditations in the Morning

"...may the meditations of my heart be acceptable in Thy sight,"

Psalm 19:14

By

Danny G. Thomas

Copyright 2015
By
Danny G. Thomas

ISBN 978-1-940609-45-4
Soft cover

All rights reserved
No part of this book may be reproduced or transmitted in any form or by any means, electronic or mechanical, including photocopying, recording, or by any information storage and retrieval system, without permission in writing from the copyright owner.

Bible versions are from KJV, NKJV, ESV, NLT, LIVING BIBLE and MESSAGE.
This book was printed in the United States of America.

To order additional copies of this book contact:

dannygthomas47@gmail.com

FWB
For Worthwhile Books Publications
Columbus, Ohio

Introduction

"Let the words of my mouth, and the meditation of my heart, be acceptable in thy sight, O Lord, my strength, and my Redeemer." **Psalm 19:14 KJV**

"Be still, and know that I am God." **Psalm 46:10 KJV**

I have found that there are two times that my mind can stay focused on God without interruption: early in the morning and when I can't sleep at night. Each of those times is a quiet time. They are times when my mind is stayed on God.

Of those two times, my favorite is the morning. It is then that I can pray, speak boldly to my God, and look into His wonderful face. It is at that time that the Lord seems to direct my mind to specific scriptures that become so meaningful at the moment. It is at that time that the Lord gives me greater understanding of passages or a fresh new light upon a piece of scripture.

Early in the morning during these wonderful times, God places people on my mind, and I feel impressed to pray for them. Often I do not know that there is a concern that these people have, but later on I discover that indeed they needed someone to pray for them. The Holy Spirit summoned me to pray with them or for them during these times.

Early in the morning, I seem to see more clearly the blessings that God has presently given my family, my friends, my acquaintances and me. All throughout the day I discover the divine appointments that I have been prepared for during those early morning hours.

It is these sweet times with my great God that compel me to write this book about some of those morning thoughts. I want to share them with you the reader. These are some of my thoughts of God and His presence with me early in the morning. I hope that they will inspire you and give you a new light of your life in Christ.

There is a unique word that is found throughout the Psalms. It is the word *Selah.* It has been defined as a poetical pause or, as I prefer to say, it means *think about it.* I have placed that line at the end of the following morning thoughts. That is what I would like for you, the reader, to do after you read the scripture and thoughts: *"think about it."*

I hope you find them to be a blessing. I want to make a ninety-day challenge to you. I want you to intentionally take a time in your day, perhaps early in the morning, to meditate upon God's Word. If you intentionally do this for ninety days, it will become natural for you. If it becomes natural for you it will be instinctive. It will become part of you, but it will not happen unless you take the first step to intentionally do it. So, JUST DO IT!

In His service together,
Danny G. Thomas

Dedicated

This book is dedicated to God's great blessing to me,
Barbara Sue Brewton Thomas whom I lovingly call
Bobbie.
She is my wife, my love, my confidant, and the mother
of our three wonderful Children
Justin Glenn Thomas
Jeremy Russell Thomas
Joni Lynn Thomas Hubbard.
I also include our grand children
Cadence
Coleman
Nash
Preston
Brooklyn
Eli
Micah
Emma

I wish to leave to them a great desire to serve
My Lord and Savior whom I serve and
Each Morning meditate upon His Word.

Danny G. Thomas

Table of Contents

Day 1: The Meditation of My Heart
Day 2: Top Ten Toddler Property Rules
Day 3: I Have Overcome the World
Day 4: Quotes from Presidents of the United States
Day 5: Grace
Day 6: Paraprosdokians
Day 7: Never Worry
Day 8: Actions Define Us
Day 9: Created for Fellowship
Day 10: I Can Do All Things through Christ
Day 11: Ordinary yet Extra-ordinary
Day 12: Losing Jesus
Day 13: Signs of a Pharisee
Day 14: Overcome
Day 15: Problems or Challenges?
Day 16: Prayer
Day 17: Disqualified
Day 18: What Are my Options?
Day 19: When Water Is Needed, Dig a Ditch.
Day 20: Go Ahead, and Do It.
Day 21: Sacrifice
Day 22: Don't Be Afraid
Day 23: Secure in Christ
Day 24: Suffering
Day 25: The Devil Made Me do it! Don't Blame the Devil.
Day 26: The Bible
Day 27: Faith
Day 28: I'm Happy
Day 29: Trust God and Tithe
Day 30: God's Great Love
Day 31: Persecution
Day 32: Enjoy Life
Day 33: Big Plans
Day 34: He is Here!
Day 35: Over Weight?
Day 36: Why Is It, That There Is Only One Way to Heaven?
Day 37: Dare to Obey

Day 38: Real Sin
Day 39: God Almighty
Day 40: God? Aren't We All Saying the Same Thing?
Day 41: Rulers
Day 42: National Day of Prayer
Day 43: The Greatness of America
Day 44: The Battle is the Lord's
Day 45: Calling Good, Evil
Day 46: A Success
Day 47: It's Not my Fault!
Day 48: Why is Jesus so Offensive to the World?
Day 49: I Will Never Deny You!
Day 50: My Peace I Give to You
Day 51: Problems, How Do You Deal with Them?
Day 52: The Lure of Happiness
Day 53: A World of Anger
Day 54: Rest in the Lord; Do Not Fear
Day 55: Are You Happy Where You Are?
Day 56: Have You Been Authorized?
Day 57: I Got Trouble!
Day 58: Enough
Day 59: Ignorance of the Law Is No Excuse
Day 60: Am I Suggesting an Answer or Seeking an Answer?
Day 61: Just Leave Me Alone; I Can Do This on My Own
Day 62: The Storms of Life
Day 63: Practical Atheist?
Day 64: That Narrow, Starlit Strip
Day 65: What Will You Do?
Day 66: Which Way?
Day 67: For Unto You Is Born This Day a Savior
Day 68: Too Little and Too Insignificant
Day 69: For Such a Time as This
Day 70: To Feel the Power and Love of God
Day 71: There Were Three Men
Day 72: A Blessing to the Nations
Day 73: Be Still
Day 74: The Lord's Day
Day 75: Hey! This World Is Rotten!
Day 76: Where Is Heaven and Who Is in It?

Day 77: Count It All Loss
Day 78: Wow! What a Wicked World!
Day 79: Go Ye Therefore!
Day 80: Random Acts of Kindness
Day 81: Is Something Bothering You?
Day 82: Know What You Believe
Day 83: Contented
Day 84: Eternal Vigilance
Day 85: Like What You Do
Day 86: A Bully
Day 87: We Are Pleasing to God When We Rejoice and Sing
Day 88: Is Anything Happening?
Day 89: Commit to Faithful Men
Day 90: Life Verses

Day 1:
The Meditation of My Heart

"Let the words of my mouth and the meditation of my heart be acceptable in Thy sight, O Lord, my strength, and my Redeemer." **Psalm 19:14**

Do words matter? Have you noticed how public officials and various leaders of our world quibble with various nuances of words in order to justify, or should I say, mislead others? They say something that everyone knows is an actual and deliberate lie. Have you further noticed how those who have been given the responsibility of check and balance tend to accept those obvious lies? I am of the opinion that if it is necessary for one to say, "What I meant to say was" or "I just misspoke" and then add another lie to what has just been lied about by saying, "I didn't say that," the meditations of the heart are being exposed.

Well, words do have meaning and meaning matters. If words don't matter, nothing can be solved. Jesus tells us that the words from our mouth are an expression of what is in our heart. *". . . What you say flows from what is in your heart."* **Luke 6:45 NLT.**

It was Ralph Waldo Emerson who wrote: *"Thought is the seat of action. The ancestor of every action is thought."*

If our words matter, then God's Word matters much more. God does not misspeak or say that which He does not mean.

God's Word is sure.
Gods' Word is final.
God's Word is true.
God's Word reveals what is in His great heart.
God's Word is His will and it will be done on earth in the same way it is done in heaven.

Through God's Word He launched the universe into existence and all that is within it **(Genesis 1)**, and it is by God's Word that judgment and wrath are enacted.

How do thoughts and intentions get into your heart? They enter through the eye gate. That which you see enters your mind, what is in your mind is retained, and what is retained is that which you meditate upon or ponder and considered doing. If you meditate long upon that which you have seen, it can become part of your heart and what is in your heart is expressed in actions. So, if you want your actions to be right, your meditation must be right.

King David said in **Psalm 139:23 & 24,** *"Search me, O God, and see if there be any wicked way in me."* The search was not for God to discover something that was hidden to Him but to reveal to David that which was hidden in David's heart and unknown to David. Perhaps it was something in which David was in denial. God had already written down in His book all the thoughts and actions of David's life, and David needed to be reminded of them or they needed to be revealed to David in order for David to be the man that he wanted to be: A man after God's own heart.

There is a chorus that many Christians learned as a child:

> *"O be careful little hands what you do,*
> *O be careful little hands what you do,*
> *For the Father up above is looking down in love,*
> *O be careful little hands what you do.*
>
> *O be careful little eyes what you see,*
> *O be careful little eyes what you see,*
> *For the Father up above is looking down in love,*
> *O be careful little eyes what you see.*
>
> *O be careful little feet where you go,*
> *O be careful little feet where you go,*
> *For the Father up above is looking down in love,*
> *O be careful little feet where you go."*

That little chorus contains words that matter. They are simple words of wisdom. Yes, words do matter for words express that which is in our heart.

Watch your heart. Watch your words closely. They matter and they have meaning. Do not be flippant in what you say. If you dream of sin and imagine sin, when given the opportunity you will find yourself indulging in sin. If you have not done so, it is because you just have not had the occasion to sin yet. If you are thinking about it, it is just as great as committing the sin because you have meditated upon it in your heart.

Is this you? Ask God to forgive you of that sin and to cleanse you of that unrighteousness, and then you will be acceptable in His sight.

The whole earth, of which Satan is its prince and power, and all that is in it is against you. They are waging war upon your mind. So fight, put on your armor, and stand. Don't go another day allowing sinful imaginations to accumulate in your mind and soul. You would not allow garbage to collect in your living room would you?

Think about it. *Selah*

Day 2:
Top Ten Toddler Property Rules

"But I say, walk by the Spirit, and you will not gratify the desires of the flesh." **Galatians 5:16 ESV**

What is the most important thing to you in life? What is your major goal in life? How do you see yourself in relation to those around you? I have heard it stated that life is like a toy box, the one with the most toys at the end of life is the winner.

Things and stuff seem to mean a lot to most everyone. But that is a selfish goal; it is a goal that is all about me. I think the desires of man are best portrayed in these rules, which are called "The Rules of The Toddler."

If I like it, it's mine.
If it's in my hand, it's mine.
If I can take it from you, it's mine.
If I had it a little while ago, it's mine.
If it's mine, you must never allow it to appear to be yours in any way.
If I'm doing or building something, all the pieces are mine.
If it looks just like mine, it's mine.
If I saw it first, it's mine.
If you are playing with something and put it down, it automatically becomes mine.
If it's broken, it's yours. (Author Unknown)

"Me first! That's mine! I want that!" These are some of the first phrases that we learn. We do not need to be taught

them; they seem to be just natural. *"The heart is deceitful above all things, and desperately sick; who can understand it?"* Jeremiah writes in **Jeremiah 17:9 ESV**

David asks God in **Psalm 51:10 KJV** to: *"Create in me a clean heart, O God; and renew a right spirit within me."* We are born into sin and therefore it is our nature. It's just natural to sin. It's just natural to want our own way. Selfishness is innate.

That is why God makes all of us, who have acknowledged that we are sinners and have repented of our sins, a new creation. After we have been forgiven, the first thing He does is to make us a new creation. He decided to do it, and it is all His doing. It is a whole new makeover. He makes us a new creature. He makes all things new.

God takes all of our sins and throws them into His purposeful sea of forgetfulness. He chooses to forget them, and they are as though they had never been committed at all. We are totally new, and the old things have been passed away. We are not what we were; we are now something totally new, a new work of divine art. We are His new creation.

Yet, there is still a problem we have to deal with after we become a new creature, and that is, we still live in the same house and are still living on this same earth. We are in a great battle of the Spirit warring against the flesh. We have our fleshly body living on the fleshly earth. We will daily have to deal with this old house until Jesus returns and gives us our new body. Then we will trade the old one for a new and greatly improved one, one that will be perfect. But until then we have to battle the sinful desires.

This war is confusing to us as we battle with our will and our spirit. **Romans 7:15 ESV** says, *"For I do not understand my own actions. For I do not do what I want, but I do the very thing I hate."*

Paul tells us to be seeking the fruit of the Spirit and resisting the works of the flesh. *"For the desires of the flesh are against the Spirit, and the desires of the Spirit are against the flesh, for these are opposed to each other, to keep you from doing the things you want to do."* **Galatians 5:17 ESV**

Until Jesus returns we will have to be involved in this great battle, but do not give up! Seek the fruits of the Spirit in order to repel the works of the flesh. The fruit of the Spirit overcomes the works of the flesh in our lives.

Expect the battle, but expect the help of the Spirit to give strength to overcome.

"If we live by the Spirit, let us also keep in step with the Spirit." **Galatians 5:25 ESV**

Think about it. *Selah*

Day 3:
I Have Overcome the World

"Here on earth you will have many trials and sorrows. But take heart, because I have overcome the world." **John 16:33 NLT**

Albert Einstein has said: *"We live in a dangerous world not because of the wicked people on it but because of the good people who do nothing about it."*

Peace is what mankind seeks, but he is unable to get hold of a lasting peace. We want lasting peace, enduring peace. In war we try diplomacy, but diplomacy will not work unless both parties sincerely want peace. Money is unable to purchase it, a good job will not provide it, and at the time we do get it, it just does not last. What we need is an eternal peace.

This is just what Jesus has offered. He can offer it because He has overcome the world with all its natural tragedies, failures, insecurities and trials. All of its disease, heartache, calamities, and death will be ended when He comes again. He gives us peace in this world of trouble and it endures even as we are affected by this world's troubles.
John 14:27

The best news is that Jesus has something to replace the trouble. It is something new. He overcame the world and He has prepared a new earth and heaven to replace it.
John 14:1-3

If you are depending on people to bring peace, then Einstein was right. You cannot depend on good people to do anything about wickedness in this world because good people do not have the power. Even exceptional people do not have the power to make an end of evil. There has never been a person, other than Jesus, who has the power to overcome the prince of wickedness. Satan is the strong man that must be destroyed. The good news is that Satan's defeat has already been announced by Jesus, "*Be of good cheer, I have overcome the world!*"

Think about it. *Selah*

Day 4:
Quotes from Presidents of the United States

"... set the believers an example in speech, in conduct, in love, in faith, in purity."
I Timothy 4:12 ESV

President Calvin Coolidge: When he noticed a little boy looking through the gate at the White House and discovered that he just wanted to see the President, he told his security officer: *"Whenever you see that little boy waiting at the gate, wanting to see me, do not let him wait, bring him to me immediately."*

Jesus also knows that we, His little children, need to see Him, and He has made it possible for us to come in to Him at any time. We can come boldly to the very "Throne of Grace." We can come immediately.

Dwight D. Eisenhower said: *"There are no victories at discount prices."* The price for our sins did not come as a discount; it required the blood of Jesus Christ. *"For God so loved the world that He gave His only begotten Son, that whosoever believeth in Him should not perish, but have everlasting life."* **John 3:16 KJV**

John F. Kennedy said at his inauguration address: *"Ask not what your country can do for you, ask what you can do for your country."* Those words are lost today. It seems that all we want is something from our country. We live in a selfish society, an egotistical one, where everybody feels they are right and cannot possibly be wrong.

If anything goes wrong, it most certainly could not be our fault; someone else has to be the blame.

Jesus commissioned His followers to **go** and make disciples. Our commission is to carry the Gospel to someone else and make a disciple of that person. That is doing something for someone else at the expense of ourselves. Jesus wants us to be concerned about the souls of men, not the treasures of man. Paul said that his personal desire and prayer to God was that his brothers, Israel, would be saved. **Romans 10:1**

What is your desire? Is it your desire for your neighbor to know the Good news? Is your desire to be used of God for your family members? What about your friends? What about your enemies? What do your prayers to God sound like? Are they full of personal needs that you want God to do for you, or are you seeking what you can do for God? Ask not what God can do for you; ask what you can do for God.

Think about it. *Selah*

Day 5:
Grace

"Therefore, as one trespass led to condemnation for all men, so one act of righteousness leads to justification and life for all me. For as by the one man's disobedience the many were made sinners, so by the one man's obedience the many will be made righteous. Now the law came in to increase the trespass, but where sin increased, grace abounded all the more, so that, as sin reigned in death, grace also might reign through righteousness leading to eternal life through Christ Jesus our Lord." **Romans 5:19-21 ESV**

The very first work and purpose of grace is for our righteousness and our salvation. Grace is the act of God that makes remission of sin possible. It makes conversion, regeneration, and sanctification viable.

The preacher's part in salvation is preaching the Good News to others so that they will repent and then be converted, and forgiveness of sin is made possible. The responsibility of those listening is that they can reject the message or accept the message. The development of the new life is up to the believer. The believer must obey God's Word, have a desire to be separated from this world, and place his allegiance in Christ alone.

Christ wants us to be genuine in our allegiance and real in our lives. He wants us to do what He calls us to do and go where He calls us to go. Christ does not want us to look at what He has called someone else to do or what he or she is not doing. He want us to follow Him.

He wants us to be what He wants us to be.

I like this poem and I feel that we all can benefit from it.

Don't Be what You Ain't

Don't be what you ain't,
Just be what you is.
If a man is what he isn't,
Then he isn't what he is.

If you're just a little tadpole,
Don't you try to be the frog.
If you're the tail don't try to wag the dog.
Just pass the plate if you can't exhort or preach;
If you're just a little pebble,
Don't try to be the beach.
Edwin Milton Boyle

Think about it. *Selah*

Day 6:
Paraprosdokians

"For our sake he made him to be sin who knew no sin, so that in him we might become the righteousness of God." **2 Corinthians 5:21 ESV**

Paraprosdokians, is a big word for a figure of speech in which the latter part of a sentence, phrase, or larger discourse is surprising or unexpected. Here are a few:

I used to be indecisive - now I'm not sure.
You're never too old to learn something stupid.
If I agree with you, we would both be wrong.
We never grow up, we just learn how to act in public.
To steal ideas from one person is plagiarism, to steal ideas from many is research.
Behind every successful man is a woman; behind the fall of a successful man is another woman.
Behind every successful man is a surprised woman.

One of the greatest surprises is: *"This is a trustworthy saying, and everyone should accept it: 'Christ Jesus came into the world to save sinners' - and I am the worst of them all."* **I Timothy 1:15 NLT**

Another one is: *"Jesus love me."* and *"Behold what manner of love the Father has bestowed on us, that we should be called children of God!"* **I John 3:1 NKJV**

Why would a God, who cannot even look at sin, send his only Son to die for sinful man, just so we can go and live with Him forever in his home?

That is amazing! That is surprising!

The Amazing Love of God! You cannot love others until you understand that God loves you. He loves you unconditionally. He loves you not because of you, but because it is His nature. God is love. Check it out for yourself.

John 3:16
John 13:34 & 35
I John 4:7-21

God not only loves you, He relates to you in love:
    1. When He disciplines you, it is because of his great love for you.
    2. When He says no to a request, it is because of that love.

We need to think about His love, take in His love, and only then can we relate to His love. When we focus on His great love, then we can return His love to others.

There is also no fear in His love. His love removes all fear and makes it easy to relate His love to others confidently and without worrying about what may happen. We can live in this fearful world without fear. **I John 4:18 NKJV** says,
  "... *perfect love casts out fear ...*".

"*If you see God as He really is, in His holiness, then you cannot miss seeing you as you really are and desire to be more like Him.*" **David Jeremiah**

Think about it. *Selah*

Day 7:
Never Worry

Phil 4:6-7: *"Be careful for nothing; but in everything by prayer and supplication with thanksgiving let your requests be made known unto God. And the peace of God, which passes all understanding, shall keep your hearts and minds through Christ Jesus."*

Never worry about anything today. Wow! That is so easy to say! But it is not easy to do in our daily life. What we need to do in order to prevent worrying is to replace that worrisome event on our timeline with a moment of prayer and thanksgiving.

When we begin to offer up thanksgiving for the things that God has already done for us, worry takes a back seat. When things in the past worried us and we saw God calm those fears, it brought peace back. If we will do this, it will help us to replace our present worries with God's great peace for today. We will experience again that peace that is beyond our ability to understand or explain to someone. That is God's peace, which only He can provide. When we put that worry into the perspective of God, peace floods in, and it is an indescribable peace.

When God's peace takes over, it is greater than any worry one might have. Remember, if God is for you, what can separate you from God? Nothing! God's presence makes all those worries seem so small and ridiculous. **Romans 8:31 & 35-39**

Actually, when we allow worry and anxiety in our lives, it makes God look small in our eyes and makes Him appear to be helpless and uncaring, rather than magnificent, glorious, loving, and the all-sufficient God that He is. If you trust God with your worry, then you are allowing God to become the guard of your timeline, your help in the time of trouble, and your peace in the storm.

Keep your thoughts and emotions on Christ, and the peace of God, which passes all understanding, will invade your life.

Yes, He is a very present help in our "timeline" of trouble and worry.

Think about it. *Selah*

Day 8:
Actions Define Us

"Or do you presume on the riches of his kindness and forbearance and patience, not knowing that God's kindness is meant to lead you to repentance? " **Romans 2:4 ESV**

"If actions define us, let us be known for actions of kindness." That is a Starbucks slogan.

Vengeance belongs to God alone and it is a fearful thing to stand before an angry God; but it is His kindness is that leads us to Him and to repentance. **Romans 2:4**

Jesus told His disciples in **John 13:35** that He was giving them a new commandment to govern their lives, and it was that they should love one another. It was by that love all men would know that they are His disciples. Love is the icon of Jesus. The followers of Christ should be known by their acts of kindness and their expressions of Godly love. By this love, they know that we are followers of Christ.

Jesus tells us that we can know each other by our fruits or our actions. Our actions give us away. If our actions and works are evil, if the fruit of our life is not God's love, and if we are not living lovingly as reflections of the Holy Spirit, we appear to be like the world. Our actions must be seen as the fruit of the Spirit. That is the way we know each other and that is the way the world knows us.

The fruit of the Spirit is love, joy, peace, patience,

kindness, goodness, faithfulness, gentleness, and self-control. **Galatians 5:22 & 23 ESV**

I feel this is a big problem in our churches today. Our churches, the body of believers that gather together all over the world, often are not displaying God's love with each other. Disagreement is not unity; it is not being in one accord. One accord is an expression of God's kindness. Too often disagreement is given too high a seat in our thinking and there is a great possibility that discord will rise up against accord. Members will begin to leave, pastors will be let go, and the love and kindness that did exist will vanish.

Discord in churches is not an act of God. It is a battle, a war, a fight. None of those words are pleasing to or descriptive of God. There is no way anyone can scripturally justify discord or disagreement. What has happened is, we have defined ourselves as having the spirit of antichrist. That is hard, but it is the truth. We have shamed the body of Christ by our actions, actions that are not of Christ.
Listen to James and Peter:
> *"What causes quarrels and what causes fights among you? Is it not this, that your passions are at war within you? You desire and do not have, so you murder. You covet and cannot obtain, so you fight and quarrel."* **James 4:1-2 ESV**
>
> *"So put away all malice and all deceit and hypocrisy and envy and all slander. Like newborn infants, long for the pure spiritual milk, that by it you may grow up into salvation--if indeed you have tasted that the Lord is good."* **I Peter 2:1-3 ESV**

Think about it. *Selah*

Day 9:
Created for fellowship

"Let us draw near with a true heart in full assurance of faith with our hearts sprinkled clean from an evil conscience and our bodies washed with pure water. And let us consider how to stir up one another to love and good works, not neglecting to meet together, as is the habit of some, but encouraging one another, and all the more as you see the Day drawing near." **Hebrews 10:22 - 25 ESV**

God created man to commune with Him. God created man as a display of His glory and for His glory. God also created man to fellowship with others. *"It is not good for man to be alone."* God said, in the garden and then provided a helpmeet for him.

C. S. Lewis has said: *"If you want to go fast run alone. If you want to go far run together.."*

Christian fellowship is essential for growth in Christ. We need one another. May we never be guilty of saying: *"I don't need anyone, I can do it alone."* That is a lie! Believers do need other believers. We do need encouragement, we do need the support of one another.

We are laborers together as a body of believers with various gifts of the Spirit and God has given each of us various talents to be used with each other. These gifts and talents have been given for us to use as we labor together and with one another. We use these gifts and talents in ministry to God's glory.

I like to sign emails, texts and letters with the closing: "*In His service together*". My reason being that we are in this thing together we are a single body of believers, a church, a fellowship of believers. We are a body with ears, mouth, hands and eyes. We are strong only when we are together, when we are united together to do what God has called us to do.

Failure is not an option, if we are working together and each one doing what He has been given. Failure only is possible when we separate from that which He has for us and start to attack one another.

Judgment is not for us, it is for God alone. God does act with judgment and vengeance but only when He desires to and when He determines to do so. Each believer's concern is if he or she is doing his or her part. If we begin to look at others, soon we are likely to stop doing our part.

We need to be patient and long suffering as God is. Peter tells us that God is: *"longsuffering toward us not willing that any should perish...."* **II Peter 3:9 NKJV**

Let judgment take a hike and instead camp out in fellowship with each other. We are in His service together.

"Strive for peace with everyone, and for the holiness without which no one will see the Lord." **Hebrews 12:14 ESV**

Think about it. *Selah*

Day 10:
I Can Do All Things Through Christ

Philippians 4:13 *"I can do all things through Christ who strengthens me."*

I don't want to suffer but I will have to from time to time and I can suffer well when empowered by Christ. Through my suffering people can see Christ and know that it is Christ in me who enables me to endure suffering. As I endure all things, it is then Christ in me Who receives the glory and not me.

I can also be victorious, when I am empowered by Christ. It is through the victories that people see, it was Christ not me who won the victory. It is Christ who receives the glory through this.

If I do random acts of kindness and I am in the power of Christ, it is Christ who receives the glory for it and not me.

If I proclaim the Good News to one person or to a million and I am empowered by Christ, and millions are saved, Christ is the one who is glorified and the many are blessed by it. I think Billy Graham is a good example of this. He always gives God the glory as do Billy's children.

If someone asks me to pray for someone who is sick, in distress, in need of finances or anything else and their prayer is answered, then it is Christ who receives the glory by the answered prayer not me.

I can do all things well, whether I serve through suffering, victory, prayer, preaching, teaching or anything else. If I do all things through Christ Jesus, they will be done, it will be He Who strengthens me, it is He Who performs through me.

It is Christ Jesus Who works through me. It is Christ who gets the glory not me.

Think about it. *Selah*

Day 11:
Ordinary Yet Extraordinary

"Now unto Him Who is able to do far more abundantly than all that we ask or think, according to the power at work within us, to Him be glory in the church and in Christ Jesus throughout all generations, forever and ever. Amen.
Ephesians 3:20 ESV

Ordinary people who are controlled by their devotion to God make for a dynamic duo. The ordinary become extraordinary, dynamite that cannot fail. The average person who is empowered by God is able to do the extraordinary and supernatural or unnatural. Even things that are way beyond our wildest dreams.
Ephesians 3:20 & Philippians 4:13

Has God laid something on your heart to do for Him? Then, do it. Don't ask why, don't ask how, don't ask when, just do it. If God is moving in your life, move with Him. Great people are not great because they are great, they are great because God is great and a great God is working through them.

They didn't want to be great, they just obeyed the voice of God and He did great things through them.

Let me leave this with you: just listen to God, obey His voice and do what He says.

The first miracle that is recorded which Jesus performed was in Cana of Galilee. John recorded in **John 2.** Jesus was at a wedding and they ran out of wine. Jesus' mother,

Mary, apparently was in some sort of a way responsible for the wedding meal or she just wanted to help the people. She didn't know what to do and neither did anyone else so she turned to Jesus.

Mary informed Jesus about it and He said to her: *"What do you want me to do about it?"*
It's not my wedding feast? Mary's response was: *"Whatever He tells you to do, just do it!"* Jesus told them to fill the empty wine pots with water. What's that all about? May have been their thoughts, but they obeyed anyway. Then He told the servants to take a sample to the Master of the wedding feast. Now that was a stretch of faith there!

Well, Jesus said it and Mary said, do whatever He says to do, so they obeyed and brought the master a sample. The results was that this wine was well beyond what they had thought, the water became the best wine. Why did you save the best to be served at the last?: was the master's response.

God only does great things, not average things, not just good things but God does unbelievable and extraordinary things. Whatever God puts on your mind to do, just do it! And you will do extraordinary things.

Think about it. *Selah*

Day 12:
Losing Jesus

"And when the feast was ended, as they were returning, the boy Jesus stayed behind in Jerusalem. His parents did not know it, but supposing him to be in the group they went a day's journey, but then they began to search for him among the relatives and acquaintances, and when they did not find him, they returned to Jerusalem, searching for him." **Luke 2:42 - 45 ESV**

Have you ever been somewhere and suddenly look around and you don't see your child? I know that has happened to all of us who are parents at one time or another. If the child doesn't realize it, then he or she is not worried, they just go about doing what they were up to at the time. The parents, on the other hand, are frantic. When we do find the lost child, what a relief it is! But what often follows that feeling of relief is a stern rebuke, *"Don't get away from us again, you need to stay with us?"*

Well, Joseph and Mary lost Jesus one day and they experienced that same feeling. They looked for Him for three days, **2:46**. When they finally found Him they discovered that He had been in the Temple all the time. **Luke 2:41 - 52**

Jesus had been teaching the teachers <u>for three days</u>. *(Reminds me of something that would happen 21 years later in Jerusalem when Jesus was lost from the eyes of all for three days and then discovered).* But Jesus wasn't lost, He was doing what the Father had given Him to do.

It seems as though that should have been the first place they would have looked. Jesus was always about His Father's business, and that is what we should be about also, about our Father's business.

They lost Him but didn't know it for three days. They looked everywhere. But he was nowhere to be found. Perhaps they thought to go to the Temple to pray and ask for prayer to help find Jesus. I think God led them there. God always knows what we have need of even before we ask. But Jesus was not lost from his parents. Actually it was Mary and Joseph who were lost from Jesus.

Today, I think sometimes we find ourselves lost from Jesus. We wonder where He is. We may even think that He has left us. But Jesus will never leave us or forsake us. He assures us of that. **Deuteronomy 31:6, Heb. 13:5** *"for he has said, 'I will never leave you nor forsake you.' So we can confidently say, 'The lord is my helper; I will not fear; what can man do to me?"* **ESV**

At the time we feel alone, or the time we feel forsaken, and begin to look to Jesus, we discover He is right there with us. Our body is the temple of God after all, isn't it? We find Him right there in the same boat that we are in. He is in the same storm that we find ourselves in. He is just waiting for us to acknowledge His presence.

Jesus is not lost, He hasn't left you, you are not alone. He is with you, so don't be afraid.

Think about it. *Selah*

Day 13:
Signs of a Pharisee

"Woe unto you scribes and Pharisees, hypocrites! For you tithe mint and dill and cumin, and have neglected the weightier matters of the law: justice and mercy and faithfulness. These you ought to have done, without neglecting the others. You blind guides, straining out a gnat and swallowing a camel! **Matthew 23:23 ESV**

The scribes, Pharisees Sadducees and priests, the religious leaders of Jesus' day, were His greatest opposition in doing what the Father had called Him to do. Jesus' problem was not with the Roman government, not with the outlaws and outcast of society or any other group of people. The greatest opposition to His mission was the religious people, those groups who should have been His greatest supporters.

Isn't it sadly obvious that this still remains to be the biggest opposition to the mission of Christ today? Why is it true that the opposition that is experienced in spreading the Good News if frequently with our religious leaders? We seem to be neglecting in the *"weightier matters of justice, mercy and faithfulness" and* unyielding in our personal ideas and understand and matters of less weight?

Don't think that you are above this, because it is easy for each of us to fall into a Pharisee mentality and neglect what really matters. Here are some of the characteristics that I think of when I hear the word "Pharisee".

They made a hypocritical, outward and proud act of small and meaningless service to God.

They were defensive of their spiritual condition. They could not be wrong. They overlooked the actual reason for worship. It's all about God.

They were unmoving in breaking of the Law by others but lenient in regard to their own actions. They thought they already knew the mind of God.

They were proud of what they knew and of their ability to relay knowledge and to teach others but were themselves in great need of learning.

I like to say they were blinded by their preferred ignorance. By that, I mean they did not want to know anything different beyond that which they already knew. They were perfectly OK the way they were, and did not want any change.

Today the Holy Spirit is our Teacher, He is the One Jesus said would teach us all the things that Jesus taught. We need to be open to the teaching of the Holy Spirit, while testing the spirit that is within us. If we see any of the works of the flesh making a move in our teaching or in things that we are involved in, we must be quick to reject it. If we see the fruit of the Spirit, embrace it. **Galatians 5:16 - 25**

Open our eyes Lord, we want to see Jesus. Teach us Your ways O God!

So, think about it. *Selah*

Day 14:
Overcome

"I cry aloud to God, aloud to God, and he will hear me. In the day of my trouble I seek the Lord; in the night my hand is stretched out without wearying; my soul refuses to be comforted." **Psalm 77:1 & 2 ESV**

The psalmist cries out to God as he is in the great grip of worry and uncertainty for help and God hears that cry. We also experience many such times of struggle in our lives and we cry out to God in our grief and he hears us and he acts and he helps us to overcome those moments of life. Yes, God is faithful.

"In my moment of fear, through every pain, every fear, there's a God Whose been faithful to me." **Cymba**la This is the first line of the lyrics of the song: He's Been Faithful. What a blessing those lyrics have been to so many. It is a song of hope, trust we have in God and his great faithfulness to us.

Did you know that storms and struggles are what this earth is all about? Expect them. There is not a single person who has ever lived on this earth, who has not experienced storms and struggles. You may think that you know some whose lives appear to be storm free, peaceful, carefree, but you just don't know them.

Jesus didn't live a storm free life, He experienced trouble every day. That's what Jesus was telling His disciples in **John 16:33**. *"In this world you will have trouble."* There was no way that the disciples could comprehend the trouble that Jesus would experience in the next few days. Yet, Jesus was ready for it at that very moment and He was about to confirm it with His Father that very night. Yes, in this world we will have trouble.

That brings me to the next phrase: *"But be of good cheer, I have overcome the world."*

Though Jesus had not been crucified yet and raised from the dead, still, God's sovereignty made HIs future as sure as if it were already done. *"I have, (past tense) overcome (already) the world."* Jesus, in agony, proclaimed: *"Father, if Thou be willing, remove this cup from me, nevertheless not my will but Thine be done.'"* **John 22:42 KJV**

His purpose for coming was to do His Father's will and it was God's sovereign which was already signed and sealed and as good as delivered!

Here in Jesus' moment of distress, there was a Father who was faithful to Him in sync with the faithfulness of His Son.

So, fellow believer, be of good cheer! Jesus has overcome all. If you are in His hands, you are in good hands. You are in the hands of The Overcomer.

Therefore, stand still and hold His hand and experience His peace and victory.

If you don't know Jesus as your Savior, you are not in His hands but you can be right now. The Word of God tells us if we trust Jesus, if we believe that He is Who He said He is, and if we will admit that we are a sinner and confess our sins and repent of our sin, if we would give those sins to Jesus, then He will forgive us of all our sins and will cleanse us of all our unrighteousness and place His pure righteousness upon us. This act will make us one with Jesus. We are in Him and He is in us therefore we become an overcomer with Him.

Say: Jesus, I know I am a sinner and I repent of my sin. I am turning around right now. Forgive me of my sins, Jesus. I believe that you are the only begotten Son of God. I believe that you died on the cross for my sins and was buried and then after three days, You rose victoriously from the grave to secure my eternal life in you. I accept your gift of forgiveness and I know you will soon return to take me to be with you in paradise for all eternity.

Thank you Jesus. And it is in Your name I pray. Amen.

If you prayed that prayer and you meant it, now you are a new creation in Christ, you are an overcomer. We are more than an overcomer, we are a possessor, an heir, and a child of the King.

So, think about it. *Selah*

Day 15:
Problem or Challenge?

"Blessed be the God and Father of our Lord Jesus Christ, the Father of mercies and God of all comfort, who comforts us in all our afflictions, so that we may be able to comfort those who are in any affliction, with the comfort with which we ourselves are comforted by God." **2 Corinthians 1:3 - 4**

It's been said that if the only challenges you may have in life are those that have been thrown at you, then you are not directing your life. You are merely reacting to the difficulties of life. You are, in effect, just playing dodge ball. You are not going anywhere, you are just dodging the ball.

Problems that are worth having are those which are involved in achieving a goal that you have chosen. It is you, who made the decision to take this on. Any time you decide to accomplish a goal you must look for difficulties that will come and then you need to adjust in your life to overcome and bring that goal to reality. These difficulties are not really problems, they are merely events or challenges that stand between you and your determined victory. They are just acknowledged hindrances that must be overcome. They are the only thing that will stand between you and your vision in life.

Difficulties are not always total surprises, they can be expected, many can be avoided but there is always opposition to any goal. So expect them, be determined to solve them and carry on.

Paul tells us that we should run the race that is set before us. King David wrote in **Psalm 37:3** that we should dwell in the land and feast upon God's faithfulness there. The question is: "How do you do that?" To adapt to the situation means that you stop and ask for strength from God, then ask God for knowledge and for wisdom in the situation. Then, you press on, you commit your way to the Lord and trust in the Lord.

It is resistance that builds muscles and makes one stronger. The Apostle Paul wrote in **Philippians 3:13 - 14** *"Brothers, I do not consider that I have made it on my own. But one thing I do: forgetting what lies behind and straining forward to what lies ahead, I press on toward the goal for the prize of the upward call of God in Christ Jesus."* **ESV**

In order to overcome we must put off those things that seem to easily beset us and make us want to quit and run with diligence. **Hebrews 12:1** It is also important for us to understand that we are not all in the same race.

Some are on a sprint,
Some are in the hurtles,
Some are in the marathon,
Some are in the iron man
Some are in the relays,
And so on. So let us work on our race, the one God has assigned to us and give our all to it; We need to be all about our race and not spending our time observing what others are doing.

The question is: What have I been trained to do and called to do by God Himself? The next things is to give my all in the race or I will lose. Every race requires training, specialized training and more training. Each race demands commitment to the training and to the Coach. The training is difficult but it will give endurance.

Some races are finished quickly, some take a long time, but every race requires faithfulness and commitment in giving ones all in order to win the prize. The race is our challenge and in the challenge from the coach and the stands is: DON'T GIVE UP! NEVER GIVE UP! PRESS ON!

Look at life as a challenge not a problem. The challenge is to press on toward the goal. Never give in, never give up, keep on keeping on. Keep your armor on, use your Sword, trust you Coach and stand confidently, stand in Jesus. Having done all . . . . STAND! *"Finally, be strong in the Lord and in the strength of His might. . . And having done all stand firm."* **Ephesians 6:10 - 14 ESV**

So, think about it. *Selah*

Day 16:
Prayer

"Is any among you suffering? Let him pray ... Elijah was a man with a nature like ours and he prayed fervently ... "
James 5:13 - 18 ESV

The disciples listened to Jesus pray and they wanted to learn to pray like He prayed. There was something different about His prayer that was noticeable to everyone. His prayers were powerful and always noticeably answered. They wanted to be able to pray like Jesus prayed. **Luke 11:1**

We find ourselves thinking that prayer is hard, but it is not. It may require great determination and passion but prayer is simple having a conversation with God. That is what Jesus was saying to His disciples.

I like how Jesus responded to the request: *"This is how you pray:"* and He simple gave them a pattern which we refer to as the Lord's Prayer but actually is was a Model Pray or an example in how to pray.

Teach us to pray, Lord! The model prayer makes it simple.

Let me point out one caution. Jesus said we should keep asking, keep looking, and keep knocking, we should be persistent, and sooner or later the door will be opened. Prayers are not necessarily answered the same time we pray, they are answered in the timing that God directs them to be answered. We just need to keep asking and then keep looking for the answer, don't stop praying, do all that we can and then the answer will appear.

Another caution is found in **Matthew 6:14 ESV** *"Forgive us our debts as we also have forgiven our debtors, and lead us not into temptation, but deliver us from evil. For if you forgive others their trespasses, you heavenly Father will also forgive you, but if you do not forgive others their trespasses, neither will your Father forgive your trespasses."*

I heard this somewhere: Prayer is not hard if:
    1. You believe you will be heard.
    2. You know the need.
    3. You know what to say.
    4. You know when to stop.

May I share with you what some individuals that I admire have said about prayer:

"If I had to reduce my prayer to just one thing I would pray for my child's personal relationship with the Lord Jesus, because if that's solid, most of the other stuff will settle in. Through prayer righteous parents can change the course and direction of their family. The prayer of a righteous parent can put a child's heart into the hand of the Lord, who directs it like a watercourse, wherever He pleases." **David Jeremiah**

"The prayer preceding all prayers is: "May it be the real I who speaks. May it be the real Thou that I speak to." **C. S. Lewis**

"The Lord hears! Shall He that madeth the ear not hear? **George Hebert**

"Is any among you suffering? Let him pray . . . Elijah was a man with a nature like ours and he prayed fervently . . . "
James 5:13 - 18 ESV

So, think about it. *Selah*

Day 17:
Disqualified

Do you know that in a race all the runners run, but only one receives the prize? So run that you may obtain it. Every athlete exercises self-control in all things. They do it to receive a perishable wreath, but we an imperishable. So I do not run aimlessly, I do not box as one beating the air. But I discipline my body and keep it under control, lest after preaching to others I myself should be disqualified."
I Corinthians 9:24 - 27 ESV

Shawn Minor who is an 18 times grand Rodeo champion is quoted as saying:
"I'm not afraid of dying, I'm afraid of losing."

The Christian does not need to worry about losing because the victory has already been won. We need only follow and obey and we will win a crown and not be disqualified because of not being obedient.

Paul says in **I Corinthians 9:27** *"But I discipline my body and bring it into subjection, lest, when I have preached to others, I myself should become disqualified."*

Play by the book, God's Word. Discipline yourself to obey God's Word, desire to obey God's Word. Determine that God's Word is our game book and when we live by the Book, we win. We are more than conquerors. **Romans 8:37**

Think about it. *Selah*

Day 18:
What are my options?

"Then Moses answered, 'But behold, they will not believe me or listen to my voice, for they will say, 'The Lord did not appear to you. The Lord said to him, 'What is that in your hand? He said, A staff." **Exodus 4:1 & 2**

My daughter Joni and her husband Heath are missionaries in Japan. They have three children, two boys: Eli, Micah and a sweet little girl: Emma. In August of 2014 she was expecting little Emma. Joni and Heath were in language study on top of expecting their third child. My wife Bobbie and I decided that we would go to Japan to be with Joni as she delivered Emma and take care of the boys and do the chores of the home in order to make it a little easier on them. We stayed seven weeks to help in any way that they might need.

The big job was Eli, who was four years old and Micah, who was two years old. We took them to school, which was just a block from the house and picked them up from school. I also took on the responsibility of separating and cleaning the trash to make it acceptable for the various days of delivery, which was the most difficult job of all. If you have lived there, you would understand. Everything had to be just right and there was no other option. I'll just stop right there on this subject.

Another job that I had was getting Eli and Micah ready for bed at night and ready for school in the morning. The big thing with Eli was what he would wear at night and what he would ware to school. When I would say: OK, let's get your pajamas on or clothes on, he would say: "What are my options?" There had to be options, I gave him only two, you can wear number one or number two. He liked that and so did I. There were no arguments as long as there were options. Sometimes his mom or dad would say: Eli, you have no options today, just wear what I have put out. Just do what I say! I, on the other hand, always gave options.

2 Kings 4:1 - 7 and **John 2:1-11** tell of events that are similar. **2 Kings 4** we see Elisha helping a widow woman with paying her debt by filling vessels with oil when she had little left. In **John** we see Jesus helping at a wedding to provide wine when there was no more wine left. The answer to the problem was to do what was asked. There were no other options left.

The truth here is when we pray and ask God for a need we need to "do whatever He tells you." **John 2:5** or "borrow vessels, not too few." Obedience is the only one correct answer. We have a single choice to make, there are only two options, to obey or to disobey. As Joshua purposed to the Children of Israel in **Joshua 24:15** *And if it is evil in your eyes to serve the Lord, choose this day whom you will serve, whether the gods your fathers served in the region beyond the River, or the gods of the Amorites in whose land you dwell. But as for me and my house, we will serve the Lord."*

Doing what God asks is not always easy, it is not always what we were thinking when we prayed. If we fall short of His Word or ignore His Word we will forfeit an answered prayer. God wants us to be obedient and thankful.
"Whatever He tells you, do it."

If you feel overwhelmed with too many responsibilities and challenges facing you at every turn, you may feel that you are running out of options and doing life on empty. This is probably what the wife of the prophet who died felt. She was desperate and in financial trouble to the point that she was in danger of losing her sons and everything she had to her creditors. She seemed to be helpless with no options but there was one and it stood before her and she did not know it.

When Elisha asked her what she had in her house, her response was truthful... Nothing, nothing, that is except a small jar of oil. What help could that be? What help? It was the answer, the other option. That nothing was just what was needed. Her limitations were turned into abundance. All that was needed now was to be obedient. As she obeyed God she discovered that little and small works big time when we add into it God.

God likes the illogical or ridiculous. Many times the illogical and ridiculous are only seen by us as ridiculous because they are beyond the natural mind, beyond the earthly bounds. We see things with limited vision, but God has total vision, "Omni-vision". He sees things as He wants them to be. This goes beyond what we ask or think, well beyond even our wildest dreams. Our wild dreams are old hat and simple to God, they are easily done by Him. *"Is there anything too hard for God?"* **Jeremiah 32:27**

Have you noticed that all the bastions of knowledge today, our colleges and universities, label God's Word as a myth, merely "ridiculous and beyond their reason"? They are right, because creating a world, universe and all of creation by a mere spoken word is way beyond human reason, it is way beyond the wildest dream of any human; it is impossible!

But Jeremiah addressed this thought in **Jeremiah 31:17** *"O Sovereign Lord! You have made the heavens and earth by your great power. Nothing is too hard for you!"* **NLT**

So, when in life you feel overwhelmed and there is nothing left to do, there is nowhere to turn? Look up? Focus on an option that will really work, we have the option of God. May He always be your first option not your last resort. If you wait to call on Him, don't, you are only providing worry a foot hold and will experience suffering needless worry.

You do know that God is a very present help in time of trouble, don't you? He is always there in the midst of our trouble patiently waiting for you to press the help button. He not only is able to give you a solution to your problem, He is the only solution.

Remember, If God be for us, who can be against us.
Romans 8:31

Think about it. *Selah*

Day 19:
When water is needed, dig a ditch.

"And he said, Thus says the Lord, Make this valley full of ditches. For thus says the Lord, You shall not see wind, neither shall you see rain; yet that valley shall be filled with water, that you may drink, bo th you and your cattle, and your beast. And this is but a light thing in the sight of the Lord: He will deliver the Moabites also into your hand."
2 Kings 3:16 - 18 NKJV

In **2 Kings 3** Israel, Judah and Edom had joined forces to battle Moab. Even with their combined forces they did not have the provisions to win the battle. The war with Moab lasted beyond their provision and they ran out of water for their army and animals. They were at a total loss for answers and did not know what to do, having reached the point after great defeat. It was at this point that King Jehoshaphat of Judah asked the question: "Is there a prophet of the Lord around?". Elisha, was the response of one of the servants of King Jehoram of Israel. I wonder why the King did not have that information. They were away from God, they were not in tune with God.

When they found Elisha and told them about their problem, Elisha was upset with the kings so he commanded them: *"Bring a musician to me."* Seems unusual doesn't it? Sometimes we can sing and play songs of praise and worship and in this time, God soothes our minds. As the musician played, God spoke to Elisha with the answer: *"Dig ditches and I will fill them with water."* Now that really seems ridiculous.

They weren't ditch diggers they were Kings and military men.

God's answer may not seem credible for the solution at the moment but His solution summons an action from us, it reveals our faith and our trust in God not in the deed. The action is not the credible thing, God is the one who is credible. Therefore, we should trust God, we should do just as He requests. The answer is actually in the act of obedience and faith and without faith it is impossible to please God. At all times we must be obedient, at all times we must trust and display our trust in God?

In this story, the people didn't have the power to overcome their problem but they could obey God and dig ditches and only God could provide the water. The digging of the ditches is not what produced the water, it was their obedience as an act of faith, the filling the ditches with water was the results of their faith and brought about God's blessing.

Therefore, if God gives you a vision, do what you can with what you have. Seek God at all times and then wait and watch. Hold out your hands and He will fill them with that dream.

Think about it. *Selah*

Day 20:
Go ahead and do it.

"And I am sure of this, that He Who began a good work in you will bring it to completion at the day of Jesus Christ."
Philippians 1:6 ESV

If God has called you to do something, do it. What He has called you to do is not based upon your ability, it is totally based upon His sufficiency, power and supply to you. What may keep you from doing what God has asked of you is what you are looking at, it's your reliance upon your ability. When you look at yourself you can't see God.

Well, it's not about you, it's about Jesus being faithful to you. May I assure you, you can trust Him, fellow believer, so pick up your faith and go in faith, faithful to follow Christ. If He called you, you are ready now. Go ahead and do it.

Billy Graham said this:
"Someone has observed that there are only three days in a week over which we have no control yesterday, today and tomorrow. We only have this moment in time to prepare for eternity. . . . If you think you can clean up your past to make preparation feasible, your efforts are futile. You can't change your past, but you can change your future."

In **Hebrews 13:8** we read: *"Jesus Christ is the same yesterday, today and forever."* He can be trusted and He does not change His mind. God can take care of all those things that are beyond our control. So don't worry about yesterday, Jesus knows all about yesterday.

Don't worry about the future, He holds the future in His hands. Today is the day you can do something about. Give the uncertain days to Jesus, and obey today. Jesus will make an eternal difference if you allow Him to. Now is the day, now is the accepted time. Go ahead and do what God has asked. Give it all to Jesus.

Someone has said: *"Sins masterpiece of hopelessness is overshadowed by God's masterpiece of forgiveness, in mercy and grace."* Mercy and Grace take care of every short coming we may have had or will have.

Philippians 4:19 *"And my God will supply every need of yours according to his riches in glory in Christ Jesus."* **ESV**

Think about it. *Selah*

Day 21:
Sacrifice

"Through Him then let us continually offer up a sacrifice of praise to God, that is, the fruit of lips that acknowledge his name.. Do not neglect to do good and share what you have, for such sacrifices are pleasing to God." **Hebrews 13:15 &16 ESV**

Jesus is our sacrifice for sin and He is the final sacrifice for sin but He expects us also to be a sacrifice, not for sin but we must sacrifice all to follow Him. He wants us to give our all for Him and to Him. We must give up all, and after we have done that, we must pick up our cross and follow Him. He leads in the way, as we follow Him. We aren't to do things our way but seek God's way and in Gods will.

I don't know if I am the only one, but it seems as though I hear a lot of pastors, preachers and Christian leaders encouraging followers of Christ to ask for things to be added to their lives to make life more enjoyable. The reason for this, most likely, is we are looking for things we can keep rather the things we can do for Christ. Rather than giving up things in our lives in order to follow Christ, we build bigger barns to hold what we picked up along the way.

God is our supplier and He can supply all things, but don't you think our need should be for doing the work that God has given us to do? Maybe we should ask ourselves the question, is our need that we have been praying for preventing us from following Christ as we should and doing His will? Are our request preventing us from achieving and doing that which God has called us to do in life?

Maybe we should ask ourselves this question: Do I have a cross to bear? Jesus tells the believer that each one has a cross to bear. Jesus put it this way: *". . . If any of you wants to be my follower, you must put aside your selfish ambition, shoulder your cross, and follow me."*

"Then Jesus said to His disciples, If any of you wants to be My follower, you must put aside your selfish ambitions, shoulder our cross, and follow me. If you try to keep your life for yourself, you will lose it. But if you give up your life for Me, you will find true life. And how do you benefit if you gain the whole world but lose your own soul in the process?" **Matthew 16: 24 26 NLT**

Jesus said that in this world we will have trouble serving Him but not to let that bother us because He has already overcome the world. **John 16:33** He is the victor and conqueror, we are following Him and are more than conquerors, we are His children! That is well worth the sacrifice.

Do the cares of this world bother you? Well, they bother me but I want to take my eyes off the cares of this world and focus clearly on the Caretaker, our Supplier. Giving up things or "sacrificing things" in this world is really not a loss, it is a gain. We don't want to gain the world, we want to gain eternal life in Christ. What is the brief moment of trouble in exchange for an eternity of joy.

Think about it. *Selah*

Day 22:
Don't Be Afraid

Matthew 10:28 Don't *be afraid of those who want to kill you. They can only kill your body; they cannot touch your soul. Fear only God, Who can destroy both soul and body in hell.*

Don't fear? How?

Don't look around, that makes you fear.

Look up that gives you peace.

<u>Fear</u> means you have <u>no answer,</u> no hope and have insecurity, and no peace.
Jesus <u>is the answer</u> and answers bring <u>hope,</u> hope gives <u>peace</u> and contentment.
Hope is <u>faith</u>
Faith produces <u>no fear</u>
If you are in God's hand, there is no need to worry about time running out. Time means nothing to God for God is timeless.

Mark 4:40 ESV *"Why are you so afraid?" "Have you still no faith?":* Jesus asked His disciples.

Franklyn D. Roosevelt encouraged the American people after the attack on Pearl Harbor: *"The only thing we have to fear is fear itself."* Fear is a debilitating thought that prevents people from accomplishing that which they desire to accomplish. The fear factor we must all face but it needs not be the conquering factor. We must remember the only great fear is recorded in **Hebrews 10:31** *"It is a fearful thing to fall into the hands of a living God."* **ESV** But if God is for us, who can be against us, who can bring a charge against us if we are defended by God? No one and nothing.

Jeremiah describes what it is like to fall into the hands of a living God in **Lamentations 2:3** *"All the strength of Israel vanishes beneath His fury. The Lord has withdrawn His protection as the enemy attacks. He consumes the whole land of Israel like a raging fire."*
NLT

Now, that is fear! But the truth is God has not created us for fear but for peace. Fear only comes apart from God. Get close to God and all fear will vanish. God stands with us and clutches us with His great and mighty hand of peace, but we must acknowledge Him first. When we see Him and acknowledge His presence in our lives, it is then that we experience His peace that passes all understanding.

So, why do you fear? Where is your faith?

One of my favorite songs is one that Tommy Walker has written: I Have a Hope. One line of that song goes like this:

"My God is for me, He's not against me!
So tell me whom then, tell me whom then shall I fear?
He has prepared for me great works He'll help me to complete.
I have a hope, I have a hope."

The believer has a great Hope and that hope is Christ Jesus, our Lord and Savior.

What is it that has you frightened and trembling with insecurity? How can a child of the living God feel insecure? Only if he takes his eye off his Hope. Don't fear. Trust your enduring Hope!

Think about it. *Selah*
Day 23: Secure in Christ

"Are not two sparrows sold for a penny? And not one of them will fall to the ground apart from your Father. But even the hairs of your head are all numbered. Fear not, therefore, you are of more value than many sparrows."
Matthew 10:29 - 31 ESV

Ethel Waters was one of the favorite singers during the early years of the Billy Graham Crusades. The Song that she sang so eloquently and everyone loved to hear her sing was: <u>His Eye is On The Sparrow</u>.

I love the lyrics of that song:

Why should I feel discouraged? Why should the shadows come?
Why should my heart be lonely and long for heaven and home,
When Jesus is my portion? My constant friend is He:
His eye is on the sparrow, and I know He watches me.
His eye is on the sparrow, and I know He watches me.

I sing because I'm happy, I sing because I'm free.
His eye is on the sparrow and I know He watches me.
Civilla D. Martin

You can be sure, confident and feel secure in the face of trials, difficulty or loss. Even while all your plans may fail you have no need to worry because Jesus is our portion in life and our constant friend is He. *"If His eye is on a sparrow then I can be confident and secure that He is watching and caring for me."*

I am glad that God loves the sparrow and he loves all His creation. Why would he not love them, he made them and said: "It is good". But as much as he care for the birds that are beyond our numbering on this earth, he loves us more. He love you so much that he sent His only begotten Son to die for you. Now that is love, isn't it?

Since I have taken God's Son as my Savior, he now is my supply, he is my source, he is my defender, He's my strength and my friend; He is my God Who cares for me. *"Not even a sparrow, worth only half a penny, can fall to the ground without your Father knowing it. And the very hairs on your head are all numbered. So don't be afraid; you are more valuable than a whole flock of sparrows."* **Matthew 10:29 - 31 NLT**

Think about it. *Selah*

Day 24:
Suffering

"Others suffered mocking and flogging, and even chains and imprisonment. They were stoned, they were sawn in two, they were killed with the sword. They went about in skins of sheep and goat, destitute, afflicted, mistreated-of whom the world was not worthy- wondering about in deserts and mountains, and in dens and caves of the earth. All these, though commended through their faith, did not receive what was promised, since God had provided something better for us, that apart from us they should not be made perfect." **Hebrews 11:36 - 40 ESV**

It was Dr. Edward Judson, the son of Adoniram Judson, who said while speaking at the dedication of the Judson Memorial Church in New York City:

Suffering and success go together. If you are succeeding without suffering, it is because others before you have suffered; If you are suffering with succeeding, it is that others after you may succeed."

The freedom that we enjoy as a nation has come because of the suffering of those who came before us. The beautiful churches in which we worship are the fruit of the suffering of those who paid the price before us.

As I read **Hebrews 11** I think history is repeating itself. The truth of the matter is, suffering for the cause of Christ has never let up. Today with our massive means of instant communication, we see suffering for the cause of Christ more readily. But, still, no one really cares. This world is not worthy of those believers, so God has taken them.

Paul writes in **2 Corinthians 1:3 & 4** *". . . who comforts us in all our affliction, so that we may be able to comfort those who are in any affliction, with the comfort with which we ourselves are comforted by God."*

What is it that you have suffered and been afflicted for those who will come after you? What price have you paid? Are you a giver or a taker? Givers are sufferers, they are those whom God has used to be His good hand on others.

Suffering and affliction develop endurance, it is a sign of dependability, it brings about confidence for others who will experience suffering in the future. It brings about comfort to know that God will always be with us in the very grip of suffering.

I Peter 4:19 *"So if you are suffering according to God's will, keep on doing what is right, and trust yourself to the God who made you, for He will never fail you."*

There are no victories that do not require endurance, struggle and suffering of some degree. Jesus has suffered as the final sacrifice for sin but there remains suffering that we can expect in life. There are sacrifices that we will continue to have to make.
All these, though commended through their faith, did not receive what was promised, since God had provided something better for us, that apart from us they should not be made perfect."

Think about it. *Selah*

Day 25:
The Devil Made Me Do It - Don't blame the Devil.

"Therefore, just as sin came into the world through one man, and death through sin, and so death spread to all men because all sinned." **Romans 5:12 ESV**

Satan, the Devil did give Adam and Eve the opportunity to sin and when given the opportunity, they took it. Satan is the author of sin but He isn't the blame for our sin, we are. So, don't blame the Devil for your sin. You are to blame, you alone hold the guilt. The Devil didn't make you sin, you chose to sin.

The Bible says for all have sinned. *"He that believeth on him is not is condemned but he that believeth not is condemned already because he hath not believed in the name of the only begotten Son of God."* **John 3:18** Sin is a personal choice, and we must accept the responsibility for it. For all, that includes me, have sinned.

There are many ways to sin. Sometimes we sin and know it, that is purposeful, intentional sin and we must repent and fall down before God in repentance. Repentance is making a U-TURN, it is a changing of direction. We turn from that sin and turn to God.

There are also times we sin and don't realize that what we are doing is sin. That is unintentional sin or we unknowingly sinned. Like the saying: Ignorance of the law is no excuse. Unwittingly sinning is still sin and we are guilty of it. King David asked the Lord, to search his heart to see if there was any wicked or sinful way in his life and to make that sin known to him. **Psalm 139:23 & 24** We too need to ask the Lord to search our hearts and see if there is any wicked and sinful way in us and then lead us in the right path of righteousness.

We also have those times of confusion and besetting sins, where we determine not to sin and end up doing what we really didn't want to do at all. **Romans 7:14 & 15** *"I don't understand myself at all, for I really want to do what is right but I don't do it. Instead, I do the very thing I hate. I know perfectly well that what I am doing is wrong, and my bad conscience shows that I agree that the law is good. But I can't help myself, because it is sin inside me that makes me do these evil things."* **NLT**

Still there are also other times when God may lead us to do something and we refuse or just don't do it or we know that we should do something but we choose not to do it and if we don't do it, it becomes sin to us. **James 4:17**

What is sin? Sin is falling short of the glory of God, missing the mark of perfection. Sin is anything that falls short of what God expects or asks. **Romans 3:23**

Every person is guilty for his or her own sin, we are to blame. Satan may be the founder of sin but we are the doer of sin. We sin against God, against others and against ourselves.

The Devil didn't make me do it, I chose to do it and I alone am to blame. Until we accept personal responsibility for our sin, sin will reign in us. **Romans 6:12 & 13**

That is the bad news but the Good News is Jesus came to completely take away all our sinfulness and unrighteousness and offers to place His own righteousness upon us. He took the punishment for my sin upon Himself and gave me a gift of eternal life. He has done this for you too.

You won't ask forgiveness for your sin until you recognize you are personally responsible for your sin and then ask forgiveness of your sin.

Think about it. *Selah*

Day 26:
The Bible

"All scripture is breathed out by God and profitable for teaching, for reproof, for correction, and for training in righteousness that the man of God may be competent, equipped for every good work." **2 Timothy 3:15 & 16 ESV**

The Bible is God's revealed word. It is His personal letter to mankind, and that is me and that is you and that is your neighbor. In the Bible we have described His plan for the redemption of mankind from the grip of sin. The Bible gives us a look at God's great love, holiness, grace and mercy. The Bible shines with the glory of God. It is the light that shines in darkness. It is truth, it is knowledge and wisdom.

The Bible gives reason for peace in the midst of the storm. It gives comfort in the grip of danger. It gives hope for the future and eternity. It answers our questions of life and creation. It does not offer defense because it is truth and truth is fact. The Bible remains true through the testing of human reasoning of the past coming out triumphant and will continue to outlast the challenges of the future.

Billy Graham has said: *"There are many bibles of different religions; there is the Mohammedan Koran, the Buddhist Canon of Sacred Scripture, the Zoroastrian Zend-Avesta and the Brahman Veda ... They all begin with some flashes of true light, and end in utter darkness. Even the most casual observer soon discovers that the Bible is radically different.*

It is the only Book that offers redemption for us and points the way out of our dilemma."

The Bible reveals to us God's mind and determination in carrying out His plan. *"He is not willing that any should perish but that all should come to repentance."* **II Peter 3:9**

"For He has made Him who knew no sin to be sin for us that we might be made the righteousness of God in Him through Christ Jesus our Lord.
II Corinthians 5:21

The B I B L E yes that's the book for me,
I stand alone on the Word of God
The B I B L E!   BIBLE!

Think about it. *Selah*

Day 27:
Faith

"Now faith is the assurance of things hoped for, the conviction of things not seen. For by it the people of old received their commendation. By faith we understand that they universe was created by the world of God, so that what is seen was not made out of things that are visible."
Hebrews 11:1 - 3 ESV

What is faith? Faith is hope and trust. Our faith is observed by others as we live out our lives. Faith is the basic and foundational substance or material for our mind-set in life. It is by faith that we act and do and it was by faith that the believers of old gained their credibility and proved their faith as real. It is the very material for living our lives.

Faith is our evidence, both direct and substantial evidence of our hope in life and for our eternal life. Faith is our hope of heaven, it is our main proof of God.

Faith is how we can explain things with boldness. It is our visible evidence for our invisible God. It is how we prove that God creates out of nothing, He merely spoke things into existence. It is our confidence in this present life and for tomorrow and for eternity.

The world knows us by our faith:

    They notice what we believe: That is our doctrine.

They notice how we communicate with other believers and God: Worship

They notice how we see others and live among them in our actions: That is

Biblical view of morality and life.

The believer lives by faith and exhibits his faith as he lives out his life.
Faith comes from God but that faith does not remain the same in us. Faith must be exercised, it will either grow or it will begin to weaken.

Faith is strengthened by prayer, with our fellowship of believers. Combining our faith with the faith of other believers and through the reading of God's Word we become confident in our faith. Faith gives meaning to life and keeps us from becoming weary in well doing. Faith is contradicts what we see it is not dependant on natural events it is dependant upon God and it confirms our future.

"Now faith is the assurance of things hoped for, the conviction of things not seen."

Think about it. *Selah*

Day 28:
I'm Happy

". . . blessed [happy] is he who trusts in the Lord."
Proverbs 16:20b *ESV*

Happiness is a choice. If you base your happiness upon environment, riches, friends, family health, employment or any related thing, you will not be happy long because these things are subject to change. The only sure way to be and remain happy is to choose to be happy, regardless. Because you want to be happy and you choose to be happy, then you are happy.

One of my favorite people was Ethel Waters who sang with the Billy Graham Crusades from her first appearance in 1957 at Madison Square Gardens to her last in 1976 in San Diego, California. I remember watching her sing on television. As I listened to her and watched her at the Billy Graham Crusades with my parents, she made me feel happy. What captivated me was her big smile and bubbling spirit, it reminded me of my Mammaw Thomas who was always singing and making up rhymes about us with that big smile and her bright, clear, loving and joyful voice.

Ethel Waters was not raised in a happy home nor did she have a happy environment to live in. She was a child who was unexpected and unwanted, born to a 13 year old mother who had been raped. She grew up poor, disadvantaged in the slums of Philadelphia. But she was gifted with a wonderful singing voice singing blues and jazz and became a star in Hollywood.

But life was still not happy for Ethel. They say she was very difficult to work with and very unlikable. It was late in life that she surrendered her life to the Lord Jesus and her life changed and she became happy in life.
The song she was noted for with the Billy Graham Crusade was "His Eye is On The Sparrow"

"I sing because I'm happy, I sing because I'm free." She chose to be happy and was happy. And Jesus made her free. Her future was now secure in Jesus and she had cause to be happy.

Don't let situations in life keep you from being happy, just choose to be happy. Life is much easier when you are happy. Life has more meaning when you are happy. You can make a huge difference in everyone else if you choose to be happy.

"What is the price of five sparrows? A couple of pennies? Yet God does not forget a single one of them. . . . So don't be afraid; you are more valuable to Him than a whole flock of sparrows." **Luke 12:6 & 7 NLT**

Think about it. *Selah*

Day 29:
Trust God and Tithe

"... test Me in this, says the Lord of hosts, if I will not open the windows of heaven for you and . . . . Rebuke the devourers for you . . . "Malachi **3:10 & 11 NLT**

"But I just don't make enough money in a month to pay my financial obligations. I can't afford to tithe." If I have heard that once, I have heard that statement a thousand times.

The story is told of a pastor who responded to that same statement from one of his church members in this way: *"Well, would you be willing to trust God to take care of you, tithe every month and bring me whatever bills you can't pay? Of course, said the man!*
Doesn't that seem a bit strange, said the pastor, you would trust me, an imperfect man, to care for your full needs, but you are not will to trust Almighty God, Who demonstrated His love and commitment to you be sending His Son to die on a cross for you?"

Doesn't that put things into perspective here and reveal a truth? God is the only sure thing, money isn't, wealthy friends aren't and family members aren't. A good job is not security for us. You can lose a job but you can't lose God. Only God is the only sure thing, because God cannot change. The writer of Hebrews states it this way: *"Jesus Christ is the same yesterday and today and forever."* **Hebrews 13:8 ESV**

God wants you to tithe but he wants you to trust Him and as you tithe. You do not tithe on your own, God is your benefactor. God promises that if you display your faith and trust him by obedience, then he will not only open the windows of heaven and pour down blessing upon on you but He will also rebuke the devourers in your life. No longer will the devourers invade your life and keep you from enjoying life. That is what is called a double blessing.

Let me challenge you: Though you are the reason for the financial condition you are in trust God to get you out by just tithing. God is offering you an easy out by just trusting him. All he asks of you is to obey him, and to trust him. Don't trust money, trust God. Don't look to the government to help you out, look to God. Don't hope in the lottery, hope in God. Don't live in fear and worry, live in peace, God's peace. You know that peace that you have heard about that passes all human understanding. Peace that goes beyond description and defining. God says: "Trust me on this thing, take me on a test drive, just see if I don't open the windows of heaven and do mighty things!

You know there is another part of this promise that is stated here, it's one that is almost always overlooked. The promise of God to rebuke the devourer and make your work profitable and not fail. Only God can do that!

So tithe, trust God and reap the benefits of trusting Him alone.

Think about it. *Selah*

Day 30:
God's Great Love

"God is love and whoever abides in love abides in God, and God in him."
I John 4:16 ESV

Never question God's love, embrace God's love and live in God's love. God said he loves you, what reason do you have to doubt him.

He sent His Son as the ultimate expression of his love for you.

He sent the Holy Spirit as the guarantee of his love.

He offers forgiveness of sin as the purpose of his love.

He is preparing an eternal home for those who accept his forgiveness of sin and as the extent of his love.

The hope for receiving his love is totally based upon his promise. His promise is true and his love is unconditional. You experience his love when you come close to him. As you feel his presence you feel his great love, hear his loving voice and loving heart.

Did you know God cannot change? His Word does not change so, the offer doesn't change and his love does not change. His word is ever true, ever sure and therefore can we can trust him, we can rely upon him. He is completely dependable and totally loveable. We become loving as we experience his great love.

We love him because he first loved us. **I John 4:19**

"So we have come to believe the love that God has for us. God is love. . . "
I John 4:16 ESV

"For God so loved the world that he gave his only begotten Son that whosoever believes in him should not perish, but have everlasting life." **John 3:16**

Think about it. *Selah*

Day 31:
Persecution

Matthew 5:11 *"Blessed are you when others revile you and persecute you and utter all kinds of evil against you falsely on my account. Rejoice and be glad for your reward is great in heaven for so they persecuted the prophets who were before you."* **ESV**

We hear a lot about persecution of Christians these days. It seems to be rampant, and out of control but the truth is, Christians have always been persecuted. Jesus told the people who were listening to Him that day that they persecuted the prophets long before they were born.

Persecution is just part of being a Christian, it is to be expected. Persecutions comes and goes, we find it is here and then there but persecution is always a factor in life. The thing Christians need to remember is: Persecution is but for a moment in time. God's peace is for eternity.

The reward in heaven for persecution far exceeds the pain and displeasure of the moment.
There is a comfort that Christians can depend upon in persecution and that is that God is always with us in persecution. He gives us the strength to endure persecution. Paul said that he counts it all joy to suffer for Christ.

When we endure persecution we then become the glory of God displayed to others. The Mohammed in his Koran call Christians the *"People of the Book"*, others call

Christians *"People of the Cross."* God calls us *His children.* We do have a book, the Bible, we do have a cross that Jesus commanded us to take up but God has given us, His children, a home. That is not an option for us it is reality.

"Indeed, all who desire to live a godly life in Christ Jesus will be persecuted."
II Timothy 2:12 ESV

Jesus wept and anguished over Jerusalem as He said: *"O Jerusalem, Jerusalem, the city that kills the prophets and stones those who are sent to it! How often would I have gathered your children together as a hen gathers her brood under her wings, and you would not!*
Matthew 23:37 ESV

Think about it. *Selah*

Day 32:
Enjoy Life

"Rejoice in the Lord always; again I say rejoice."
Philippians 4:4

Let me mention three phrases that many people find difficult to say, three short phrases that could make life so much simpler and less stressful if they could flow out of the mouth sincerely. Two of these three phrases I find difficult to say. These three often stand in the way of our enjoying life, those three phrases are:

1. I love you.
2. I'm sorry, I was wrong.
3. I need help.

I love you is easy for me to say to my loved ones and I say it often but "I'm sorry, I was wrong." and "I need help." cause me to struggle. I like to think that I am self-sufficient, and to admit that I am wrong is hard to swallow. The great boxer, Mohamed Allie would jokingly state: *"I have only been wrong once in my life and that was the time I thought I was wrong but wasn't"*

The reason we find these things difficult to say is that we must admit we are not independent but dependent. No one is completely independent and from time to time we must admit that we need help, we must admit that we made mistakes and we need love of others.

When we make mistakes we must learn how to correct them and not hide them. If we hide them, they will pop up again. If we recognize them as error and seek to sincerely correct them they will no longer be in the way of enjoying life.

You cannot become a Christian until you first admit you are a sinner in need of forgiveness. Once you do admit sin and ask forgiveness of sin, Jesus forgives and the sin is gone. It is as if it had never happened, total and eternal forgiveness. It is gone as far as the east is from the west. It is in the sea of God's forgetfulness. His forgetfulness is something He chooses to do. And if he determines to do so, it is so and He never brings it up again because He has decided that it no longer exists.
Now that is forgiveness.

God says to us:
    I love you
    I forgive you
    You have my help

Think about it. *Selah*

Day 33:
Big Plans

"For I know the plans I have for you, says the Lord, They are plans for good and not for disaster, to give you a future and a hope." **Jeremiah 29:11 NLT**

If you have a college aged friend or child who is a Christian or who is just getting out on their own, more than likely their favorite verse or life verse will be Jeremiah 29:11. The reason being, I believe, is that they are making plans of their own and going out on their own, in one extent or another and they are concerned about their future. They need a great hope. And that hope is Jesus.

God wants us to know that He has plans for us. He wants us to know that life is worth living when it is lived in Christ. We don't have to go through life alone, When God is with us, as we go, He already knows what is ahead of us in the going and He can be trusted to lead us.

Nothing surprises God, there is no situation or no point in time that takes Him by surprise. Before the very foundation of this world and this universe, He already knew everything **Psalm 139:16.** He knew my name and He knew your name. He knew everything we would do and say and every event that we would be confronted with. Knowing all this about me and you He still has precious thoughts about us. **Psalm 139:17 Knowing** before He spoke to us, with full knowledge of us, He says His thoughts of us are precious, and we are precious.

God is good and His plans are good, this is why He can tell us that His plans for us, which cannot be overcome, will be for a good future, not disastrous, not temporary but for our eternal good.

Though His plans are "for good", but not everything that happens on earth "is good" because this is earth, and it's not good. Why? Who is it's prince that wields power over it? It is Satan. Remember, this is not heaven, but it is not hell either.

So God tells us that He will go with us in our journey through life. He will empower us, and He will not allow anything to touch us that has not first been run through His good hand. He will, with all these earthly and temporary trials, troubles and difficulties give us all that is needed to overcome them. As we go and overcome He receives glory in the eyes of others.

Remember when Mary and Martha approached Jesus after their brother Lazarus had died? They said: *"Lord, if you had been here, my brother would not have died."* **John 11:20 & 32 When** Jesus saw them weeping, He was overcome with emotion and He asked: *"Where have you laid Him?* His great and loving heart was taken by their pain. But His plans for them was for their good, for their prosperity and for the glory of God.
They were correct in saying that had Jesus been there their brother would not have died. But this death was for God's greater glory. Jesus said, it is better for you that I was not here so you could see something greater.

These people were about to experience the awesome power of the presence of God's great glory. This event was planned before the foundation of the world, this was choreographed for their benefit and all those who were there and for us who read about it.

Don't judge the goodness of God by what is happening now. If things seem to be out of God's hands, just wait. Like Moses at the Red Sea, stand still and see the glory of God.
Yes, this earth is not all that there is. There is a future. Is God part of your future? He can be, if you let Him.

"... behold now is the accepted time; behold now is the day of salvation."
II Corinthians 6:2b KJV

Today, now is the time, life is worth living and eternal life is worth it all!

Think about it. *Selah*

**Day 34:
He Is Here!**

"... The teacher is here and is calling for you." **John 11:28**

Omnipresence, that's a big word, and it has a big meaning. It's unbelievable and impossible for created being to grasp. We cannot understand it because it is a creator thing. It is something that only God Himself can retain, something that takes a creator mind to understand.

Omnipresence means that God has the ability to be everywhere at the same time. It also includes in it the characteristic that God knows everything. The truth that He is all knowing means that He knows our very thoughts (Omniscience). He knows all our past thoughts and all our future thoughts. He hears them because He is here. Did you notice I said "our" thoughts? He witnesses them, everybody's at the same time. Regardless of where you live, where you go, God is there. You can't hide from Him, you cannot fool Him. **Psalm 139:7 - 12** *"Where can I go from your presence.. "*

He is here! He is there, He is with you and He is with me!

For the believer, this is a great comfort.
For the non-believer, this is a great caution.
For Satan, this is a reminder of something he is not, He is not Omnipresent or omniscience.

Satan cannot be by me and by you at the same time. What Satan can do is go to and fro in the world looking for things to accuse us of. He is known as the accuser of man. O yes, another thing, Satan cannot read your mind, he does not know your thoughts but God does know them.

Satan gets his information from all his angels. He does have a great host of fallen angels doing his will and creating havoc in this world. The Bible tells us that when Satan fell he took one third of the angels with him, those are his demons, the fallen angels. **Revelation 12:4**

But Satan's time is short. His sentence has already been read. His doom has already been sealed. So, he wants to do all he can to bother God's people until he is finally thrown into hell for eternity with all his buddies.

But know this, God draws the line as to what He will allow Satan to do on this earth. Satan is the prince and power of this earth and this earth is not heaven but it is not hell either. For now, Satan is on this earth and Satan is still working his devilish deeds within this earth.

It will soon end, when Satan receives his due punishment. This earth is bad but God is with us all!

He is almighty God without limit.
There is no limit to His presence,
There is no limit to His knowledge and wisdom,
There is no limit to His power,
There is no limit to His love,
There is no limit to His mercy,
There is no limit to His grace!

And He is here!

Think about it. *Selah*

Day 35:
Over weight?

"Therefore, since we are surrounded by such a huge crowd of witnesses to the life of faith, let us strip off every weight that slows us down, especially the sin that so easily hinders our progress. And let us run with endurance the race that God has set before us." **Hebrews 12:1 NLT**

Do you struggle with your weight? Are you wanting to lose weight? In these United States of America, we do tend to eat too much. I know I have a problem. I have to keep a watch on myself.

If you put a bag of potato chip beside me and leave, if you don't come back soon, they will all be gone. I have no will power to stop eating potato chips. I don't even have to be hungry, it's the idea that they are there. It's like Sir Edmund Hillary who was the first person to conquer the peak of Mount Everest in 1953, whose response to the question: Why did you want to climb Everest? *"Because it was there."* He did conquer that mountain and summit it's peak. As I reached the bottom of the potato chip bag, my only reason for consuming it is: Because it was there.

Physically and materially many of us find ourselves fat while spiritually we are dangerously weak, much too lean and extremely anemic. I think we need to work on losing physical weight and increasing our spiritual weight.

Too much physical weight can kill you and too little spiritual weight can endanger your spiritual life and wellbeing. The believer must daily exercise personally and with a fellowship of believers as well. We all must have communion with God daily that is our potatoes, bread and meat of our spiritual life.

We need times of worship and praise, quiet times of sweet communion, which is the sweets, and the desert of our spiritual life.

Billy Graham has pointed out: *"Unless the soul is fed and exercised daily, it becomes weak and shriveled. It remains discontented, confused, and restless."*

We do need to watch our physical weight but be sure to indulge in the meat and sweets of the Word and work out your own salvation, flex your muscles, run the race, reach toward the prize.

Think about it. *Selah*

Day 36:
Why is it that there is only one way to heaven?

"There is salvation in no one else! There is no other name in all of heaven for people to call on to save them." **Acts 4:12 NLT**

God is holy. God cannot look upon sin. God is pure, clean and totally undefiled. God cannot sin, He cannot do anything against His own will. God never changes therefore what He says must be done. God is sovereign and cannot be overcome. As we speak the Model Prayer we acknowledge that truth when we say: Thy will be done on earth as it is in heaven. When all is said and done, God's will must be done, on earth in the same way it is done in heaven.

The problem with mankind is our unholyness and unholyness is ungodliness. Ungodliness is anything that is not like God. Sin is not like God. Satan is the author and inventor of sin and mankind was invaded by and overcome by sin in the garden. The result of sin is the demand that a death penalty must be made for sin. The death penalty was an eternal death. Satan and Mankind were sentenced to eternal death as a punishment.

Since God was attacked, He responded with the sentence of death. But God still was not willing that any should perish and He was long suffering. **II Peter 3:9** What needed to be done was a pure sacrifice for man's sin. That sacrifice must be something pure and holy to be put in the place of that sin.

Man couldn't do anything because he was polluted with sin. Angels could not do anything because they were not human, they were spirits. Man had to pay the price but there was no man. Therefore God did something unbelievable, something only the mind of God could conceive. He would make a new creation by taking His own Son, Who knew no sin at all and making Him to be sin, mankind's sin for mankind. In the place of sinful mankind stead, God freely offered an alternative, an exchange, man's unrighteousness and sin for Jesus' righteousness. **II Corinthians 5:21** Wow!

God the Father would send His Son to be born a man, yet retain His Sonship as God's only begotten Son. The Father made man a new creation, something impossible for mankind. This is a God thing, It would be all God's doing, all His workmanship, it is all His idea. **Ephesians 2:8 & 9**

It was the only way, there was no other name that could do this. *"And there is salvation in no one else, for there is no other name under heaven given among men by which we must be saved."* **Acts 4:12**

So Jesus came, God loved the world so much that He was willing to send His only begotten Son. He would be the complete sacrifice for sin. The complete payment for sin. Now, mankind can accept this free gift or he continue to reject the love gift of God.

Think about it. *Selah*

Day 37:
Dare to Obey

"Finally, brethren, whatsoever things are true, whatsoever things are honest, whatsoever things are just, whatsoever things are pure, whatsoever things are lovely, whatsoever things are of good report; if there be any virtue, and if there be any praise, think on these things.. . I can do all things through Christ which strengthens me."
Philippians 4:8 & 13 NKJV

A. W. Tozer has said: *"A man who is elated by success and cast down by failure is still a carnal man. At best his fruit will have a worm in it.*

Faith dares to fail. The resurrection and judgment will demonstrate before all the world who won and who lost."

Our success or failure in life will not be defined by the things that we have done but by how faithful we have been to what Jesus actually called us to do. Many a man or woman has built great buildings, colleges, universities; many have given huge amounts of money for needs all around the world, many have won battles and wars, and accomplished great feats and deeds. It just took great men and women to do those things. But only Christ can change the destiny of man. That's a God thing, only God can do that.

Jesus' followers are his hands, hands which He empowers to do things well and way beyond their natural ability. The only thing He asks of us is that we obey. We need not know how things will work, we are only to obey. Though we are insufficient for the task in our own minds and think that we can't do what He has asked, it all changes when we factor in Christ. When we exercise faith in Christ and obey him, it all change. Jesus wants us to trust Him, so dare to obey him.

Faith is doing something that is doomed for failure unless God steps in. That is a God thing, that is daring thing, that is totally trusting God, it is relying on God and on God alone. And God cannot fail.

When you become cast down, when you can only see what is around you right now, look up, the answer is above you, don't quit, never say quit, never say can't, never give up, never give in. Press on, keep on doing with a joyful heart.

Success comes in God's timing not ours. Time doesn't mean anything to God because he is not bound by time and space but, timing is everything to God. It is in the fullness of time that God acts. *"But when the fullness of time had come, God sent forth His Son, born of woman, born under the law."* **Galatians 4:4**

Trust God, dare to obey and you will not fail.

Think about it. *Selah*

Day 38:
Real Sin

"For God sent Jesus to take the punishment for our sins and to satisfy God's anger against us. We are made right with God when we believe that Jesus shed his blood, sacrificing His life for us. God was being entirely fair and just when he did not punish those who sinned in former times. And He is entirely fair and just in this present time when He declares sinners to be right in His sight because they believe in Jesus." **Romans 3:25 & 26 NLT**

Charles Spurgeon has written: *"Men who do not play with words and call themselves sinners can call upon the Lord. The inn of mercy never closes it's doors upon such, neither weekdays nor Sundays.*
Our Lord did not die for imaginary sins, but his heart's blood was spilt to wash out deep crimson stains, which nothing else can remove."

If you call yourself a poor lost sinner that means that you have insufficient funds to make right the sins of your life, you have lost all sense of direction, you don't know where you are now and you have no hope of righting yourself. You sin and that makes you a sinner.

Perhaps you may consider yourself like Paul, "the chief of sinners". Those were not frivolous words that Paul uses. He persecuted the church and thought he was doing God a great favor.

He stood at the stoning of Stephen showing his approval. The radical terrorist of today have nothing on Paul, because he was their chief, he was their leader. These were real sins that Paul was talking about, not imaginary sins. The early church bears witness to Paul's sins: *... He who used to persecute us is now preaching the faith he once tried to destroy."* **Galatians 1:23 ESV**

If the blood of Jesus could cover Paul's sin it will cover yours. I think this is one reason the Holy Spirit led Paul to write the words in **Romans 5:20** *"Where sin did abound, grace did much more abound."* This means that God's "desire" to forgive you of all your sin is greater than your "ability" to sin.

God forgives sin. God destroys sin, He vanishes sins away He makes them disappear to the point it's as if they had not been committed, they never existed. Is that not an awesome thought? We sin because we are sinners born in a sinful world. We sin real sins, grievous sins, sins against those we love, sins against mankind, sins against God. And the blood of Jesus Christ was shed for **real sin** . . . . Your sin.

Would you like to see a miracle? If you will confess your real sin, you will receive real forgiveness and receive in the place of your real sin, real righteousness, the holy and pure righteousness of Jesus Christ.

Think about it. *Selah*

Day 39:
God Almighty

"Holy, holy, holy, is the lord God Almighty, who was and is and is to come!
Revelation 4:8

Here are some words that are used to describe God?

Supremacy: Nothing higher

Sovereign: The right to be always in control. What He says is law.

All powerful: Always able to control.

All knowing: Always knew everything, never had to learn anything and was never wrong.

Always was: Firsthand knowledge on everything.

Always will be: Reliable

Always present: Never leaves, God with us. Eternally now.

Always the same: dependable

Supernatural: Well above the natural.

Creator: Made all things.

These attributes are what it takes to be God.

If all these things have to be true, then there can only be one true God. I challenge you to match them up with those who are claimed by others to be God. If you believe in God, then all of these characteristics must be true about your claim or you are believing in a god.

To know God personally will make your life secure because you are in His hands therefore, you have no legitimate cause to worry, because God tells us:

"Is there anything that God cannot do?" **Genesis 18:14**

"If God is for us who could be against us?" **Romans 8:31**

"For with God nothing is impossible." **Luke 1:37**

If you do not know God but would like to know God there is a prerequisite, faith. *"But without faith it is impossible to please Him, for he who comes to God <u>must believe that He is</u>, and that He is a rewarder of those who diligently seek Him."* **Hebrews 11:6**

If you don't believe there is a God, you are just living by chance, the only way you have to explain things is by chance. Surely you must at least believe in a prime mover? What or who would that be? You need to find out.

You might say: You are wrong! There is no God. Let's say you are right and there is no God. Will believing that there is a God hurt me? How will believing that there is a God and that I know Him personally, affect me when I die? But, If I am right, and you are wrong; there is a real God and you do not know Him, will that hurt you? How will that effect you when you die? Do you feel that is something you should consider?

I have discovered this as my personal experience compared to those around me, life is so much easier with God.

He brings peace, comfort, He gives hope, He provides answers to the questions in my life. He is the Way, He is the only Truth, and He is true Life, and He has promised me life eternal.

Think about it. *Selah*

Day 40:
God? Aren't we all saying the same thing?

"How can you believe, when you receive glory from one another and do not seek the glory that comes from the only God? **John 5:44 ESV**

Today we see governments, and various groups trying to revise God. Religions through out the world are trying to unite as one. Many of our religious leaders are advocating that everyone just come together and set up a new world set of values, a new united religion. Why? They say Christianity is no longer relevant to the world's people.

Many people today proclaim that religion is the very reason for all wars and fights all throughout history. You know what? They are right in one sense, but Christianity is not a religion; Christianity is a way of life, Christianity is a faith, a belief and a trust in the person, Jesus Christ.

Jesus says He is the only way to heaven. Above Him there is no other name given among men where by a person can be saved we read in Acts 4:12. We read in many places in the Bible where God claims that He is the only God and beside Him there is none other. **Isaiah 44:11, Deuteronomy 32:39**

This world is not heaven, it is the place of dominions, powers, workers of iniquity ruled by Satan for now. **Ephesians 6:12**

Jesus is preparing a new place for us, a new earth and a new heaven. This world is a place of trouble for now. But that will change. Jesus came to save mankind from this world and from eternal death, not to set up a kingdom on this earth.

Remember what Jesus told Pilate in **John 13:33**? *"So Pilate entered his headquarters again and called Jesus and said to Him, 'Are you the King of the Jews?' Jesus answered, do you say this of your own accord, or did others say it to you about me?' Pilate answered, Am I a Jew? Your own nation and the chief priest have delivered you over to me. What have you done? Jesus answered, My kingdom is not of this world. If my kingdom were of this world, my servants would have been fighting, that I might not delivered over to the Jews. But my kingdom is not of the world."* **ESV**

Perhaps religions are saying the same thing, but Jesus has commissioned Christians to proclaim the Good News of His Kingdom, the Kingdom of Heaven. That is not what others are saying, no, we are not all saying the same thing.

Religions do change but the Word of God does not change, and Jesus remains the same, yesterday, today and forever.

Think about it. *Selah*

Day 41:
Rulers

"He that ruleth over men must be just, ruling in the fear of God. And he shall be as the light of the morning, when the sun riseth, even a morning without clouds; as the tender grass springing out of the earth by clear shining after rain." **II Samuel 23:3 & 4 KJV**

Billy Graham tells of watching President Eisenhower kneel in a chapel in Geneva and ask God for divine guidance in the deliberation that would soon take place, just before the "Big Four Conference".

I like that and wish that prayer would be a priority of world leaders today. If that were to be true, I believe we would see more lasting peace, if even one would seek the mind of God, and would have a desire to rule in justice and the fear of God.

It seems to me that we used to have statesmen in these United States of America who led us to be the shining light to the world. But somewhere along the way we have gotten off course. No longer do we see brightness in our future or do we hold up that light for the rest of the world. Storm clouds have risen and continue to rise everywhere all day long, all week, every month and all through the years.

Leaders today seem to be more concerned about party loyalty than national unity strength. We define ourselves today with terms that express divided loyalty. We describ ourselves as hyphenated Americans not

Americans. We seem to have more dedication, pride and loyalty to our various ethnic groups than to our nation. We find ourselves today a divided nation. We take pride in declare that our strength is in our diversity not in our unity. The truth is that strength cannot come through division but rather unitedness. It's not our differences that make us strong, it is what we have in common, those things that with which we agree matter most. I fear that our division will only bring a great downfall.

If we sought God's direction, that would be our coming together, it would be our seeking the will and guidance of God. God cannot be found in discord, He is found in accord. When we come together in the same mind. God is not the author of confusion and He is not the reason for division. Solomon lists discord with the things that God hates. **Proverbs 6:16 - 19** When people are in accord, one accord, it is then that miraculous things begin to happen.

We won't see the world come together until and we experience a rebirth in unity, until we see men and women born again through Christ Jesus and become at peace with God and men. It is only then will we have peace with one another and live together in one accord. We will find leaders that want to rule in the fear of God today? Let us pray for our nation.

Think about it. *Selah*

Day 42:
National Day of Prayer

"Now on the twenty-fourth day of this month the people of Israel were assembled with fasting and in sackcloth, and with earth on their heads. And the Israelites separated themselves from all foreigners and stood and confessed their sins and the iniquities of their father." **Nehemiah 9:1 & 2 ESV**

After the Union army was defeated at the Battle of Bull Run, President Abraham Lincoln declared a National Day of Prayer and Fasting. These are His words:

"It is fit and becoming in all people, at all times, to acknowledge and revere the Supreme Government of God; to bow in humble submission to His chastisement; to confess and deplore their sins and transgressions in the full conviction that the fear of the Lord is the beginning of wisdom; and to pray withal fervency and contrition, for the pardon of their past offenses, and for a blessing upon their present prospective action.

And whereas when our own beloved country, once, by the blessings of God, united, prosperous and happy, is now afflicted with faction and civil war, it is peculiarly fit for us to recognize the hand of God in this terrible visitation, and in sorrowful remembrance of our own faults and crimes as a nation and as individuals, to humble ourselves before Him and to pray for His mercy . . . That the inestimable bond of civil and religious liberty, earned under his guidance and blessing by the labors and sufferings of our fathers, may be restored."

After losing the second Battle of Bull Run, Lincoln wrote his famous Meditation on the Divine Will: *'The will of God prevails. In great contests each party claims to act in accordance with the will of God. Both may be, and one must be wrong. God cannot be for and against the same thing at the same time. In the present civil war it is quite possible the God's purpose is something different from the purpose of either party--and yet the human instrumentalities, working just as they do, are of the best adaptation to say this is probably true--that God wills this contest, and wills that it shall not end yet. By His mere quiet power, on the minds of the now contestants, He could have either saved or destroyed the Union without human contest. Yet the contest began. And having begun He could give the final victory to either side any day. Yet the contest proceeds."*

What grips me here is the sincere heart of Lincoln. He leaves the opening toward God that he, the President of the Northern States, he himself could be wrong. He was asking God to search His heart. It also displays that God, is a God not bound by time but given to His own timing. God does things in the fullness of time, at the right time, right on time.

God did have a purpose here and there were great men of God on both the North and South. At the end of that great and awful war, these United States remained United and would be used of God, in the not too distant future, to bring and insure peace to an unsettled world. Oh that our leaders today were as Lincoln was.

Through all these present and uncertain times in which we live today, we can be sure that our God remains to be a very present help even in this time of trouble.

"Blessed is the nation whose God is the Lord, the people whom He has chosen as His heritage." **Psalms 33:12 ESV**

Think about it. *Selah*

Day 43:
The Greatness of America

"How beautiful upon the mountains are the feet of him who brings good news, who publish peace, who bring good news of happiness , who publish salvation, who says to Zion, ' Your God reigns' " **Isaiah 52:7 ESV**

The French Historian Alex de Tocqueville, wrote these famous words:

'I sought for the greatness and genius of America in her commodious harbors and her ample rivers - and it was not there..
In her fertile fields and boundless forests and it was not there..
In her rich mines and her vast world commerce - and it was not there.
In her democratic Congress and her matchless Constitution - and it was not there.
Not until I went into the churches of America and heard her pulpits flame with righteousness did I understand the secret of her generousness and power. America is great because she is good, and if American ever ceases to be good, she will cease to be great."

A great nation has a great God, it is the great God who has made the nation great. A great people cares for the souls of other people. A great nation is known for its great righteousness. Because of its display of righteousness to people, the world exalts them as a great nation. King Solomon writes in **Proverbs 14:34 ESV** *"Righteousness exalts a nation, but sin is a reproach to any people."*

The world needs some good news today, it needs something that would give it reason to be happy.

People need the Lord and that is the charge that Christ gave us to Go and teach all nations making disciples and baptizing them in the name of the name that is above all names. That name is the name of Jesus. We need to publish the good tidings of great joy, a Savior who is Christ the Lord.

"Be still and know that I am God: I will be exalted among the nations, I will be exalted in the earth, The Lord of Host is with us; the God of Jacob is our fortress. Selah."
Psalm 46:10 & 11 ESV

Think about it. *Selah*

Day 44:
The Battle is the Lord's.

Matthew 10:34 - 42 *"Do not think that I am come to send peace on earth: I came not to send peace, but a sword. . . . "*

Have you ever considered the danger of spreading the Good News? In Moslem countries it is against the law to bring the Good News. You can lose your head for having a Bible. In these countries, to convert to Christianity and become a follower of Christ carries with it a death sentence.

Why should we to go into all the world in countries where it is against the law to share Christ? How is it possible for Believers there to lead a new found friend to become a follower of Christ and all the while knowing that their newfound faith could lead to their death?

The answer is a simple one and this is it: The believer and follower of Christ must be an obedient servant and Jesus said go, so we go not wondering how or why. It is not our responsibility to evaluate the mind of God but to obey the commandment that He gave us and do it. We carry the Gospel, we are not responsible for carrying out the Gospel that is what the Holy Spirit does. We are to plant the seed, water the seed and till the land and then harvest what God does in the field.

The protection of the believer is God's responsibility and God will do as He wills to do, He does as He pleases. In **Matthew 25:14 - 30** Jesus gave the parable of a great man going off and leaving three of His servants in charge of various areas of his business. He gave one five talents, let's say five million dollars, another two talents or two million dollars and the other one talent or one million dollars. Each was given assets to manage according to his own ability to manage.

When the man returned he called the three in to see how they did. The first two had doubled theirs. The servant who had been given five million dollars now had ten million and the one with two million dollars now had four million. To those the master was well pleased and gave them added responsibility or a raise for their faithfulness.

It was a totally different story with the third servant. He had been given one million dollars, not because he was less liked by the master but because one million was the amount that was what he was well capable of managing.

When the servant reported to the master, he returned to the master the same one talent or one million dollars. This infuriated the master. What this servant did was nothing, he just hid the money. Why would he do that? He reports to the master that he knew that the master was a hard business man and so he just hid it. The master questioned him by saying, why didn't you just put it in the bank and at least it would draw interest? The unfaithful servant was capable of handling the responsibility he had been given but he was unethical and too lazy to do his job and no profit labeled him as unprofitable to the master.

This resulted in the servant being fired and the one millions dollars that he had was rewarded to the one who now had ten million dollars. Why? Because he had proven himself to be the most profitable servant. To whom much is given, much is required but it is also true that to whom little is give, it is required of servants to be faithful.

What that says to us is that each of us has various abilities and we are to perform those abilities to the best of our ability or according to the amount of our faith that we have. Some have great faith, some little faith and then there are those with no faith. No faith means no work. To whom much is given, much is required and it is required of servants to be found faithful. **Luke 12:48 & I Corinthians 4:2**

Strive to be found faithful. Oswald Chamber has noted:
'We must be faithful to Jesus Christ, not our own ideas about Jesus Christ but to Jesus Christ Himself.
Faithfulness to Jesus means that I must step out even where I cannot see anything. But faithfulness to my own ideas means that I must clear the way mentally.
Faith, however, is not intellectual understanding; faith is a deliberate commitment to the person of Jesus Christ, even when I can't see the way ahead."

In obedience to the command of God, believers are to do all that we can with that which we have been given. Remember we are not to evaluate or rationalize the validity, safety or human profitability of going, just go, just be faithful. If God calls us, God equips us with His ability, our job is to use the equipment that He gives us.

What is the call of God to us? The call is to proclaim to the world the Good News that Jesus died for the ungodly, that is me, you and everyone else. Now that is good new! God has placed the message in our hands and expects us to be faithful in working until He comes again and we want to hear Him say to us: "Well Done, thou good and faithful servant! You have been faithful in a few things now I will give you greater things to do. So, lets take it and not look back or around. If God is for us, who can be against us and in Him we are more than conquerors.

Think about it. *Selah*

Day 45:
Calling Good, Evil

"Woe to those who call evil good and good evil, who put darkness for light and light for darkness who put bitter for sweet and sweet for bitter! Woe to those who are wise in their own eyes and shrewd in their own sight! Woe to those who are heroes at drinking wine, and valiant men in mixing strong drink who acquit the guilty for a bribe, and deprive the innocent of his right. **Isaiah 5:20 - 23 ESV**

Sounds like the world we live in today, doesn't it. Our world is totally upside down. The values we once considered of great value were sought after are no longer considered an asset. In their place we have placed crudeness and evil and they are those traits which our world craves and strives to acquire.

Billy Graham has noted that *"People today hate when they should love, quarrel when they should be friendly, fight when they should be peaceful, wound when they should heal, steal when they should share, do wrong when they should do right."*

Our world wants peace but wants to achieve peace with conditions, it wants its own way. We want to feel safe but we are unwilling to do what is actually required to live safely. We have safety belts but don't want to wear them. We go to great extremes to make our lives free of danger yet permit our children to have all sorts of violent video games in their hands and call that good. We won't take our children to church because we call church bad. We buy CD's of singers and rappers whose words quickly become imbedded in our children's minds and feel that is good. We allow unborn babies be killed and call that good because the happiness of the mother of that baby is more important. We won't allow prayer in our schools and institutions and call that good but we will allow teachers and professors with anti-government, anti-God, anti-social ideas to teach our children and call that good. We won't allow a teacher or professor who is Christian and conservative to give a student a Bible and call that good, yet, allow radical terrorist writings required reading. And on and on it goes. We proclaim peace and safety when there is a clear and present danger around.

Jesus is the only real answer, so look up! Your redemption is very near! The time is short my fellow Christian, make the most of your day! There is so much to be done and we must be faithful! Jesus said: *"Why do you call me good, there is only one that is good."* **Matthew 10:18**

Think about it. *Selah*

Day 46:
A Success

Trust in the Lord and do good, dwell in the land and befriend faithfulness. Delight yourself in the Lord, and He will give you the desires of your heart. Commit you way to the Lord; trust in Him, and He will act." **Psalm 37:3 - 5 ESV**

Henry Blackaby has said: *"God will not lead you beyond your present level of trust and obedience. He will retain you to your present level of trust and obedience."*

That is so true. My Dad and Mother had me retained in the first grade of school, although I actually passed. Why did they do that? Because they knew that I did not have the basic skills that I needed to build upon. Not having those needed basic skills and fundamental tools would lead to greater discouragement and failure.

The same is true in our Christian faith, our faith is a building process, a little faith leads to greater faith. Unless you gain the basic truths of life in God you cannot grow to a greater understanding of God and able to do greater things. Peter told the early churches in Asia Minor that they should desire the sincere milk of the Word that they might grow. **I Peter 2:2**

The writer of Hebrews told the Hebrew Christians in **Hebrews 5:12 - 14** *"For though by this time you ought to be teachers, you need someone to teach you again the basic principles of the oracles of God. You need milk, not solid food, for everyone who lives on milk is unskilled in the word* *of righteousness, since he is a child. But solid food is for the mature, for those who have their powers of discernment trained by constant practice to distinguish good from evil."* They needed to be retained.

Chuck Colson has said: *"It was during the lonely days of prison, I learned to know God."*

Alexander Solzhenitsyn often said: *"Blessed prison, 'twas there I met God."*

To be retained does not mean that you lost or failed, it means that you have more to learn.

Joseph was retained in prison to position him for leadership of a nation that had him imprisoned, and for sustaining his family and people in the future.

It was in retained prison that Paul wrote to the Philippians Church: *I count it all joy.*

While retained on the Isle of Patmos John wrote Revelation

John Bunyon wrote Pilgrims' Progress while retained in prison.

Solzhenitsyn was impassioned while retained in prison

Colson met Jesus as he was retained in prison

Dietrich Bonhoeffer enlightened the world while retained in prison. He wrote; *"Who stand firm? Only the one for whom the final standard is not his reason, his principles, his conscience, his freedom, his virtue, but who is ready to sacrifice all these, when in faith and sole allegiance to God he is called to obedience and responsible action: the responsible person, whose life will be nothing but an answer to God's question and call."*

What about you? Have you been retained! God has a reason for it. Just stand firm, stand still and understand. Make sure that after you have done all you know to do, just stand although you may be constrained, retrained and retained.

Think about it. *Selah*

Day 47:
It's not my fault.

"Yes, Adam admitted, but it was the woman you gave me who brought me the fruit, and I ate it.' Then the Lord God asked the woman, 'How could you do such a thing?' The serpent tricked me,' she replied. 'That's why I ate it.' "**Genesis 3:12 & 13 NLT**

"'Tweren't me what did it, 'twere my brother!" That was a funny little statement I used to jokingly say when I was a child. But that is no joke in reality. Nothing seems to be our fault does it? There's always someone else we can place the blame on. No one is willing to take the blame for wrong. No one wants to face the facts. The court docket is filled with people suing other people for their own short comings or wrong actions.

The truth is that each person has a personal choice they must make all through life. Sometimes we make right choices, and life is good and then there are wrong and bad choices and we experience tension and strife in our lives.

It was Joshua who put the question before the nation of Israel: *"Choose you this day whom ye will serve; whether the gods which your fathers served that were on the other side of the flood, or the gods of the Amorites, in whose land you dwell: but as for me and my house, we will serve the Lord."* **Joshua 24:15 KJV**

All throughout the Bible and all throughout time there have been choices that people had to make and must

make in the future. The only person to blame for that choice is the one that made it. When I make a choice, I am responsible for the choice I made. We must quit blaming society, quit blaming our environment, our family, our plight in life or anything else.
I have to deal with things, I must take responsibility for the choices in which I have made.

The believer has a big advantage, an Associate and Advisor. We have a personal Counselor, the Holy Spirit, Who is with us always. Peter refers to him with words of encouragement in **James 1:5** *"If any of you lacks wisdom, let him ask God, who give generously to all without reproach, and it will be given him."* **ESV**

Jesus tells us to ask and we will receive even the words as to how to answer others. *"When they deliver you over, do not be anxious how you are to speak or what you are to say, for what you are to say will be given to you in that hour. For it is not you who speaks, but the Spirit of your Father speaking through you."* **Matthew 10:19 & 20 ESV**

The best choice one can make is the choice for God. When you choose God, you choose His wisdom, you choose His power, you choose His abundance. You choose someone Who can be nothing but faithful, cannot fail and will never leave you, never forsake you.

Why would anyone want to choose otherwise?

Think about it. *Selah*

Day 48:
Why is Jesus so offensive to this world?

"If the world hates you, know that it has hated me before it hated you. If you were of the world, the world would love you as its own; but because you are not of the world, but I chose you out of the world, therefore the world hates you. . . Whoever hates me hates my Father also. If I had not done among them the works that no one else did, they would not be guilty of sin, but now they have seen and hated both me and my Father." **John 15:15 - 24 ESV**

Blindness is one reason the world hates Jesus. They just can't see Him or they don't even know He is here.

Deafness is another reason that they hate Jesus. They just can't hear Him above the noise. Satan has blinded their eyes and stopped their ears.

They see, but they cannot see His love for the world
They hear but they cannot understand His grace and mercy.
They know they have sin and lacking in life but refuse to acknowledge their sin and shortcoming and excuse it all by that which they do see and hear, which is a lie. The way that seems to be right to them. What they see, hear and understand is what they are allowed. They are a slave to the whims of Satan their prince and power.

I witnessed this in North Korea. All the people know is what the government allows them to know. They only see what the government allows them to see. They only hear what the government allows them to hear.

It all seems right to them, but that does not make it right.

Jesus warned us that He came into the world to bring a sword. A weapon of offensive battle. The Sword is the Word and we can use it today and it was by it that the battle was won against sin and the grave. Not, the battle will be won, but the battle has already been won and Satan does not like it.

Satan's aim today is to prevent as many as possible from accepting Jesus as their savior and Lord. He doesn't want the world to see God, he doesn't want the world to hear God's Good News and he doesn't want the world to understand God's Word. He only wants them to feel OK. He only wants them to continue on down the way they are going thinking all is well. Satan wants to keep captive those enslaved in their sin, doing Satan's desires. He wants to divide as many families and friends as possible.

Our job is to be the bearer of Good News to the captive. Let us be faithful in doing that!

Think about it. *Selah*

Day 49:
I will never deny you.

"Be strong and courageous. Do not fear or be in dread of them, for it is the Lord you God who goes with you. He will not leave you or forsake you."
Deuteronomy 31:6 ESV

Have you ever heard someone say, or perhaps you have said, If I were alive in the days of Jesus, I would have been faithful, I would have never forsook or deny him. The Bible says that Peter did just that, he said it openly: *"Though they all fall away because of you, I will never fall away!"* **Matthew 26:33** All of the disciple chimed in agreeing with Peter. But when the time came, they all left Jesus and Peter openly denied Jesus.

When Peter said that, he wasn't just blowing smoke, he really meant what he said. The problem was that Peter really didn't know himself, and neither do we. If we would have been there we would have reacted just like the rest of the disciples.

We can't brag about our actions, we can only hope that we would react with the bravery that we think we have. We can overcome today if we go in the power of God and not our own. We need to understand that we are weak and insufficient on our own for the battle but in the power of God, more than sufficient. We must always strive to be in his strength alone because his strength is perfect. If we think we won't fall, then we better think again because that is just the time we are most apt to fall. **1 Corinthians 10:12 ESV**

Jesus is the only one who could predict how he would react. his only reason for coming was to do the will of the Father and was always in the hand of his Father when he died on the cross, Jesus said: *"Into Your hands I commit my Spirit."*. That is why he prayed, *"Not my will, but Thine be done."* Jesus was all about doing the Fathers will.

It was through his death that his passion was displayed and it was in his resurrection that his deity was proved. We all want to think that we will be faithful but each of us will have moments of failure in our Christian life but we can be confident in this one thing, though we may be faithless from time to time but he remains faithful. **2 Timothy 2:13 ESV** Put your faith in Christ not in yourself.

Think about it. *Selah*

Day 50:
My peace I give unto you.

"Peace I leave with you, my peace I give unto you: not as the world gives give I unto you, Let not your heart be troubled, neither let it be afraid." **John 14:27 ESV**

Jesus offers peace to us. He not only offers it to us, He leaves it with us. This peace is a great peace, it is an indescribable peace which cannot be explained. His peace just is and it never leaves us so it is dependable. It comes even when we don't expect it. I have heard so many times the witness of believers who related that peace: I don't know how or why but there was such a great peace that came upon me in that tragedy. It didn't go away, it remained.

Paul speaks of it in **Philippians 4:7** *"And the peace of God, which surpasses all understanding, will guard your hearts and your minds in Christ Jesus."* **ESV**

Isaiah writes: *"You keep him in perfect peace whose mind is stayed on you because he trust in you."* **Isaiah 26:3 & 4 ESV**

His peace comes:
in the midst of a storm,
in time of trouble,
in time of need.
It is dependable, durable, unfailing, sustaining and loving.
It cannot be explained, denied or stopped. The peace of God just is.

It is in our weakness that we experience God's peace and it gives us strength.

Thank you Lord for Your peace!

If you have received his peace you are one of his children. If you are not a believer, you can be today and you too can experience the peace of God.

Think about it. *Selah*

Day 51:
Problems, How do you deal with them?

"In the world you will have trouble, but be of good cheer. .. " **John 16:33**

Problems, we all have them. We all have to deal with all kinds of attacks upon our everyday life. Problems can be a discouragement or they can be a challenge and an opportunity for advancement.

Jesus warned His disciples about problems that they were to experience, not because they were bad but because they were in a bad world. *"In this world, you will have trouble..."*.
Trouble is going to happen, trouble is just part of life.

But we have an advantage for living in the world, we have a help button that we can press whenever we experience trouble. The best things about the experience of trouble, is that Jesus has the answer for the trouble. Not only does He have the answer but He has already overcome the trouble.

He is the "Help Button" in life or the "Google" search for the problem. Ask about it and He will guide you through it. **James 1:5**

They had already experienced that "Help Button" when they were in the storm, Jesus was with them and He had the answer, even though their faith was AWOL.   **Mark 4:40**

When problems come, don't get upset. We can be concerned but we don't need to be overcome "The Overcomer" is with us. **John 16:33 The** Holy Spirit is by us and is here for us. Don't look at the problem, look at our Helper. He will get us through.

In 1916 Ella Wheeler Wilcox wrote this poem that is has been a inspiration to millions throughout the world.

'Tis the Set of The Sail or The Winds of Fate

But to every man there openeth
A highway and a low.
And every mind decideth
Which way his soul should go.

One sails east,
One sails west,
By the selfsame winds that blow.
'Tis the set of the sails,
And not the gail's,
That tells the way to go.

Like winds of the sea,
Are the waves of time,
As we journey along through life,
'Tis the set of the sails of the soul,
That determines the goal,
And not the calm or the strife.

Ella Wheeler Wilcox

Set your sail, into the Holy Spirit (Holy Wind) and he will take you through the storm and you will gain understanding of the past and present, you will gain wisdom for the future and you will be a guide and comfort to others.

" Blessed be the God and Father of our Lord Jesus Christ, the Father of mercies and God of all "comfort", Who comforts us in all affection, with the comfort with which we ourselves are comforted by God. For as we share abundantly in Christ's sufferings, so through Christ we share abundantly in comfort too." **II Corinthians 1:3 - 5**

Keep your eyes on Christ not on the problem and He will lead you and give you peace, indescribable peace, the peace of God that is beyond our understanding and more than sufficient for anything that would confront us.

Think about it. *Selah*

Day 52:
The Lure of Happiness

"But seek first the Kingdom of God and his righteousness, and all these things will be added to you." **Matthew 6:33 ESV**

"We hold these truths to be self-evident, that all men are created equal, that they are endowed by their Creator with certain unalienable rights that among these are life, liberty and the pursuit of happiness. . . ." **Declaration of Independence**

We all want to be happy, we all would like to be free from the cares of this world but the truth is that as long as we are in this world there remains its cares. The care of this world is a duty that God gave man in the Garden of Eden: **Genesis 1:15** *"And the Lord God took man and put him in the garden to work it and keep it."* **ESV**

One way to be happy is to do what you were created to do, to be involved, to be doing something creative and worthwhile. The first duty that God gave man was to keep up and care for God's creation. When we make something better, as we take care of it, there is a since of happiness and joy associated with it. We are doing what God planned for us to do.

C. S. Lewis wrote of the pursuit of happiness as being: *"An ever-increasing craving for an ever-diminishing pleasure."* Happiness is not something that once we obtain it, we will always have it. I think it is a mindset one has, it is a choice one must continually make daily. Daily, we choose to be happy.

Jesus told us to *"seek first the Kingdom of God and all these things will be added unto you."* **Matthew 6:33**

Paul wrote in **Colossians 3:1 & 2** . . . *seek the things that are above where Christ is , seated at the right hand of God. Set your mind on things that are above, not on things that are on the earth."* **ESV**

God gives us joy and if you have joy a bi-product of joy is happiness. The Joy of the Lord is lasting and secure. *The joy of the Lord is our strength*, the Bible tells us in **Nehemiah 8:10.** It is worth noting that Nehemiah wrote this in the midst of rebuilding the walls of Jerusalem. He was busy. When Sanballat and Tobiah and Geshem and all their buddies tried to distract Nehemiah with a distraction, Nehemiah was involved in something and he was making a difference in Jerusalem as he led the people in rebuilding the walls. He had something to do that God gave him to do. His response was: *"I am doing a great work and cannot come down. Why should the work stop while I leave it and come down to you?* **Nehemiah 6:3**

Nehemiah was busy doing what God called him to do, he was making a difference, he had been encouraging the people to work, they were happy and he was happy in the work.

If you are doing what God has called you to do, that is not work, that is joy. Don't let others rain on your party. Keep up the work you have been called to do, and be happy!

One last thing about the Joy of the Lord. There is joy in knowing that whatever we might need in doing the work is readily available just for the asking. Whatever we need, supplies, strength, power, knowledge or wisdom, is sitting on ready. Anything that would challenge our joy in service can be overcome just for the asking. **Philippians 4:21; James 1:5**

God wants us to ask and when we ask He will supply. Asking is important in happiness. The more we ask, the more we pray and the more we pray, the more we experience God's faithfulness to supply. The more we know about God the more we ask for things according to His will and the cycle continues. The more we see His supply the less we are discouraged and the less we are discouraged, the more content and happy we are.

"Truly, truly, I say unto you, whatever you ask of the Father in my name he will give it to you. Until now you have asked nothing in my name. Ask and you will receive, that your joy may be full." **John 16:23 & 24 ESV**

Think about it. *Selah*

Day 53:
A World of Anger

".. he who used to persecute us is now preaching the faith he once tried to destroy." **Galatians 1:23 ESV**

What in the world is happening to this world? How can people do what they are doing today and feel they are doing God a service? We are going backwards not forward. We see people being burned alive, mutilated and tortured in barbaric ways. Genocide is something that people brag about openly and pray to their god to bring it about. We find that Christians are hated by barbarians and the elite alike, both the ignorant and learned are of the same mindset.

There are war and rumors of wars. Families are fighting with each other, children are divorcing their parents, homes are being divided, anger is displayed daily on the television screen and "preachers" are fanning the fire. We see churches in discord and division though they know God is not the author of division and He hates discord. We are finding gangs to be a big problem in our neighborhoods and schools. Why? Discontent and greed is at the root.

James 4:1 - & 2 *"What is causing these quarrels and fights among you? Isn't it the whole army of evil desires at war within you? You want what you don't have, so you scheme and kill to get it. You are jealous for what others have and you can't posses it, so you fight and quarrel to take it away from them ..."* **NLT**

Jesus said: *"Happy are the meek; for they shall inherit the earth."* **Matthew 5:5 ESV**

The believer needs to employ the fruit of the Spirit and put off the works of the flesh, **Galatians 5:16 - 26** Meekness is not weakness, it is strength restrained for a weaker person. It is not considered an attribute that anyone desires to acquire today. Jesus is the answer and His love is the weapon.

In short, the world needs the Good News of Jesus and believers need to keep the commandment of Jesus. *"This is my commandment, that you love one another as I have loved you. Greater love has no one than this, that someone lay down his life for his friends."* **John 15:12 ESV**

Think about it. *Selah*

Day 54:
Rest in the Lord, do not fear.

"Fret not yourself because of evildoers be not envious of wrong doers! For they will soon fade like the grass and wither like the green herb. Trust in the Lord, and do good; dwell in the land and befriend faithfulness. Delight yourself in the Lord, and He will give you the desires of your heart. Commit your way to the Lord: trust in Him and He will act." **Psalm 37:1 - 5 ESV**

Rest is a song that Steve Green used to sing many years ago, and it is one of my favorite songs. The melody and words just mesh so well and it brings about the feeling of rest, trust, peace and contentment. We all need rest from time to time in this hectic world that we live in.

Today, we have all types of miraculous tools that have been invented to make life easier and stress free but somehow, they seem to have made our lives all the more hectic and impersonal.

What we really need is contentment, but we are not content. We want too much and the more we want the more congested our lives become and the more competition we find with our quest of more. Completion brings battles and the battles have with them greed, worry, distrust and evil desires. Our only delight is for more in life, and so we find ourselves fretting over life.

Psalm 37 encourages us to delight in the Lord, not things, and then He will give us the desires of our heart. We find our fretting in life, becomes mere fleeting and a momentary distraction.

"Fret not, it only causes you harm." **Psalm 37:8 NKJV**

Anne Graham Lotz has made this observation and wrote this in her book, <u>Why?</u>

"I have learned to rest. If my father goes to heaven, this week, this month, this year or remains a long time; If my husband regains his health and becomes independent, or returns to the hospital in another series of crises; If my relationships are gloriously reconciled or remain broken; if my prayers are answered in the way I have prayed or continue to give no indication they have been heard. If my ministry dyes up or flourishes; If my financial resources remain sufficient for my needs or evaporate in medical expenses. Like Habakkah, I will rejoice in the Lord as I let go of what I want, when I want it and lie down on the arms of my Heavenly Father."

Habakkah 3:16 - 19 "*Though the fig tree should not blossom, nor fruit be on the vines, the produce of the olive fail and the fields yield no food, the flock be cut off from the fold and there be no herd in the stalls. Yet I will rejoice in the Lord; I will take joy in the God of my salvation. God, the Lord, is my strength he makes my feet like the deer's; he makes me tread in my high places.*" **ESV**

Think about it. *Selah*

Day 55:
Are you happy where you are?

"Don't get tired of doing what is good. Don't get discouraged and give up, for we will reap a harvest of blessing at the appropriate time. Whenever we have the opportunity, we should do good to everyone, especially to our Christian brothers and sisters." **Galatians 6:9 & 10 NLT**

If you are unhappy where you are serving Christ right now, be joyful to know that God has paced you there for the time being to be a light to those very people who are making you unhappy. Don't let them take your eyes and mind off what God has called you to do.

You can be confident of this thought, you are making Jesus happy where you are because it is He who called you. God placed you there, for the time being, having full knowledge of all that you would be confronted, with all the evil things that people may do. And He has provided what you need to accomplish that mission. You may soon have to dust your feet off for God is finished with you there and he leads you to your next assignment some where else. One more thing, you can also be confident of this added thing, Joy will come again, it is just over the horizon. Joy will burst forth with the dawn of a new day.

"... *Weeping may tarry for the night but joy comes with the morning.*"
Psalm 30:5 ESV

"I will bless the Lord at all times; his praise shall continually be in my mouth."
Psalm 34:1 ESV

Do you know what your responsibility is? It is to be the ambassador of Christ, to proclaim, to teach and admonish. Your work is not to convict people or make them respond, that is the work of the Holy Spirit to convict the hearts of man and it is the people's responsibility to respond. So be happy and faithful doing what God has called you to do. Your desire ought to be to make God happy, not people.

One of my favorite Bible verses is **II Corinthians 4:1** *"It is God is His mercy Who has called us to this wonderful work of telling His Good News to other, therefore we never give up."* **LB**

Don't give up, don't give in and don't get discouraged; because this time of trial will only endure for a brief moment. A new day will soon arise.

Keep your eyes on the Lord not on the way people respond.

Think about it. *Selah*

Day 56:
Have you been authorized?

"Not all people who sound religious are really godly. They may refer to me as Lord, but they still don't enter the Kingdom of Heaven. The decisive issue is whether they obey my Father in heaven. On judgment day many will tell me, 'Lord, Lord, we prophesied in your name and cast out demons I your name and performed many miracles in you name.' but I will reply, 'I never knew you, Go away, the things you did were unauthorized.'" **Matthew 7:21 - 23 NLT**

What an awful thing! Can you imagine playing a game with God who knows all things and think you could fool God? I wonder: "What were they thinking?" Did they not really know they were living a lie? I think they knew all the time and they thought God didn't know.

I remember many times hearing my dad, who was a pastor and preacher of the Word of God say: *"What frightens me most in preaching is preaching the real Word of God not my own idea. I always ask myself is this God's Word or my word? God holds me responsible for leading people in His Word and in His path."* **Glenn E. Thomas**

That is my concern also, it is my fear as well. I don't ever want to preach something as truth because it "seems" right to me or sounds good, I want to have the passion to preach and teach it because it "IS" The Truth. I want to preach and teach the Way that is right. Nor do I want my life to mislead someone else. The lives we live are a confirmation to what we really believe. How we daily live means much more and makes a much greater statement to others than anything we might say.

The major thing that Jesus taught is repentance of sin and it is that repentance of sin which will summons God's forgiveness. If repentance is not preached then forgiveness cannot be obtained. Repentance is the key. There are all types of things and schemes that are preached today, seldom is it that I repent.

Preach the cross, preach repentance of sin. There is no other way, we often find before us a way that seem to be a right way but it is not, it will only lead us to destruction the Bible says in **Proverbs 14:12** Listen to the still voice whispering to us: "... 'This is the way, walk in it.' " **Isaiah 30:21b ESV**

My prayer for me is that I would never abandon the way of God and The Word of God that is real authority. Jesus has given us authority in our mission, and he has qualified us for the mission.

"Giving thanks to the Father who has qualified you to share in the inheritance of the saints in light." **Colossians 1:12 ESV**

"After Jesus finished speaking, the crowds were amazed at His teaching, for He taught as one who had real authority- quite unlike the teachers of religious law."
Matthew 7:28 & 29 NLT

Think about it. *Selah*

Day 57:
Got Trouble right here in River City!

"People are born for trouble as predictably as sparks fly upward from a fire."
Job 5:7 NLT

"Ya got trouble, right here in River City!
It starts with "T" which sounds like "P" which stands for
"pool",
Right here in River City"

Those are some of the lyrics from a song in the musical **Music Man.**

It's not necessary to go to River City to find trouble. We live in a world of trouble. Sad to say but trouble is part of the fabric of life. Jesus said that in the world you will have trouble. We try to avoid trouble but we cannot. I think trouble may be more like the compost of life. Trouble stinks and when we are around trouble, we stink and we can't get to the point that we are free of it.

But trouble can be viewed in another light. Compost is something we use to cause greater and stronger garden growth. It can be viewed as the fertilizer of life that can bring added growth. It makes for a strong plant. It stinks, it's revolting, and it's rotten but makes for a better plant. We can take joy in that.

James 1:2 - 4 *"Dear brothers and sisters, whenever "trouble" comes your way, let it be an opportunity for joy. For when your faith is tested, your endurance is fully* *developed, you will be strong in character and ready for anything."* **NLT**

So, when you find yourself in trouble and in need of wisdom in dealing with trouble, then ask for help. Help will come from God, and He will freely and gladly give it. It's ours for the asking. **James 1:5**

"God blesses the people who patiently endure testing. Afterward they will receive the
Crown of life that God has promised to those who love Him." **James 1:12 NLT**

Hey, "ya got trouble?" Take the trouble to God, is using you in the trouble to make you a stronger, more competent believer. There are others who are watching you and God will use you to encourage them and he will reward you for your faithfulness.

Think about it. *Selah*

Day 58:
Enough

"Then the Lord said to Moses, 'Behold, I am about to rain bread from heaven for you, and the people shall go out and gather a day's portion every day, that I may test them, whether they will walk in my law or not. On the sixth day, when they prepare what they bring in, it will be twice as much as they gather daily.'" **Exodus 16:4 & 5 ESV**

What God offers the believer is enough for the day. We are not to stockpile or store up things on this earth. Our store house is in heaven. If we want to store up, then we are like the rich man who thought he needed to tear down his barns and build bigger barns to house all that he had stockpiled. **Luke 12:13 - 21**

What God promised us is our daily bread. His help comes one day at a time, it comes in our time of need. The purpose for storing up is that you think you will not have something in the future. We store up because we do not have the faith we need to have. Don't doubt God, just ask for the things you need today. Tomorrow will take care of it's self.

Here is a poem that I feel expresses it well:

I Wish You Enough

I wish you enough,
Enough sun to keep your attitude right.
Enough rain to appreciate the sun more,
Enough happiness to keep your spirit alive,

Enough pain so that the smallest joys in your life will appear much bigger.
Enough gain to satisfy your wanting,
Enough loss to appreciate all you possess.
Enough hello's to get you through the final good-bye.
-unknown-

The truth is, if you have Jesus in your life, you have more than enough. If you trust God, then there is no need for barns, all we need is in God's barn.

Think about it. *Selah*

Day 59:
Ignorance of the law is no excuse.

"Do not think that I have come to abolish the Law or the Prophets; I have not come to abolish them but to fulfill them. For truly, I say to you, until heaven and earth pass away, not an iota, not a dot, will pass from the Law until all is accomplished. Therefore whoever relaxes one of the least of these commandments and teaches others to do the same will be called least in the kingdom of heaven, but whoever does them and teaches them will be called great in the Kingdom of Heaven. For I tell you, unless your righteousness exceeds that of the scribes and Pharisees, you will never enter the kingdom of heaven." **Matthew 5:17 - 20 ESV**

I'm sure you have heard the saying: *"Ignorance of the law is no excuse."* well that is true. I was traveling late at night on my way to Greenville, North Carolina on Interstate 95. The speed limit had been 70 mph and I was traveling in "grace" at 75 mph. Because of my inobservance, the speed limit had been reduced to 60 mph and I was unaware of it. All of a sudden, there was this great flash of light. My response at the time was the same as yours might have been. *"What in the world was that?"*: I said to my sleeping wife. She was startled as well.

Well, I found out a few weeks later what that flash was, when I received by mail a letter which contained a picture of me behind the wheel of my car, in my droopy eyed posture. There was also a picture of my license plate and another picture of my car from a different angle. Attached to the picture album was a personal invitation for me to meet with the local judge of that town at a prescribed date. Failure to attend that meeting would result in time in jail. They were kind enough to attach a statement of what the posted speed limit was and what my personal crime of exceeding that posted limit by 15 miles an hour would be.

But, I didn't realize that I was speeding, or more correctly stated, that I was speeding by that much. My ignorance was not excuse, and it cost me $175.00. The shame was that I could have taken the 200 mile trip and stood before the judge and he might have shown me mercy and extended to me grace, but I did not go. My ignorance of the law is no excuse but ignorance of grace that could have been extended is a shame.

God's Word never changes it is law. What God expects is perfection and we are incapable of perfection. Therefore, God the Father sent His only begotten Son, Jesus Christ to offer to us His grace and mercy. Grace is offered us as an escape. We don't deserve it but His mercy and His love has offered it, and with Agape Love He extends it. Why? Because He is not wanting anyone to perish.

To live life without experiencing God's mercy and grace is a shame. The law is the law and it does not change by one iota but grace is a special gift that must be taken personally and in person, and without exception.

Yes, ignorance of the Law of God is no excuse for breaking God's Law but, what a shame that anyone would tread under foot this precious offer of God's love.

"For God sent not His Son into the world to condemn the world, but in order that the world might be saved through Him. Whosoever believes in Him is not condemned, but whoever does not believe is condemned already, because he has not believed in the name of the only Son of God."
John 3:17 & 18 ESV

Now that is Good News! Take it and share it with the world, If you don't, that's a shame.

Think about it. *Selah*

Day 60:
Am I suggesting an answer or seeking an answer?

"And when you pray, do not heap up empty phrases as the Gentiles do, for they think that they will be heard for their many words. Do not be like them, for your Father knows what you have need of before you ask him."
Matthew 6:7 & 8 ESV

In **Luke 11:9 Jesus** tells His disciples *". . . ask, and it shall be given you; seek, and ye shall find; knock, and it shall be opened unto you. For every one who asks receives, and the one who seeks finds, and to the one who knocks it will be opened."* **ESV**

The voice of the believer praying is sweet in the ear of God. He invites us to pray and he wants us to ask him for things in prayer. God wants us to seek him and approach his throne boldly and confidently. But as we ask we should be asking God not commanding.

Sometimes our children ask us for things and they can be demanding at times for those things. They are actually telling us to do something, not asking. They want to get their way and if the demand is not met they tend to get their feelings hurt.

I feel quite confident in making this assumption: There is at least one thing that all of us have asked the Lord to do in our life and our faith is becoming weak because it has not come about yet. We have asked, and it has not happened yet, so we have our feelings hurt. God does it for others but not for me: perhaps we might think.

Maybe, what is missing here is for me to quit trying to lead the Holy Spirit in my life by giving him suggestions in what to do and start allowing the Holy Spirit to do what the Father sent him to do in my life; which is help, counsel and teach.

God will direct our life if we let him. If we think he isn't perhaps we are standing in front of him and saying, "Well, come on, do what I asked." Maybe he is waiting for us to wait be still for a moment and just listen and then to follow him, our Guide, our Teacher, our Comforter.

Think about it. *Selah*

Day 61:
Just leave me alone, I can do this on my own.

"You say, 'I am rich. I have everything I want, I don't need a thing! And you don't realize that you are wretched and miserable and poor and blind and naked."
Revelation 3:17 NLT

If you don't need help, you have no need of a Helper. If you are already comfortable, you have no need of a Comforter.

If those things are true in your life, then you are out of fellowship with God and definitely out of His will.

I think that is exactly where many of us find ourselves today. I think that is where many of the church of Jesus Christ in America find ourselves. We can't see our need or do we acknowledge it nor are we grateful for what God has given us. What is blocking our view?

Francis Chan has said: *"If you have no need for the Holy Spirit, you are too self-sufficient and too comfortable and definitely not where you can be used by the Holy Spirit."*

The reason Jesus sent the Holy Spirit as our Helper is that we cannot do what He has asked us to do alone. We need help and that is why the Holy Spirit inspired Paul to encourage us with these words: When we are weak, we have the strength to do what God has asked of us. Because we can't do God things by ourselves we must rely on Christ Who strengthens us. It is because of our lack of supply and our lack of power that God has offered to supply all our needs through Christ Jesus.

If you think you can do things on your own, then that is exactly what you are doing: "things on you own". If you can do it on your own, then that is a human thing that a lot of people are able to do on their own. But if you want to do things that are beyond yourself you need God. If your desire is to be left alone, you are a poor and an unhealthy part of the body of Christ. Believers need each other and believers need Christ. If you want to be healthy and part of the body of Christ, then you need to listen to what He is saying, and go where He is leading. It's not about you.

Think about it. *Selah*

Day 62:
The Storms of life

"And they went and awoke Him, saying, Save us, Lord; we are perishing." **Matthew 8:25 ESV**

In Matthew 8 we find the disciples in great danger. In the grip of this great storm, they found themselves overcome with fear. They began to be overcome with doubt and tears if distress flooded their eyes like their boat was being filled with water. As they begin to bail the boat, Jesus was asleep on a pillow in that boat.

They woke up Jesus and said: master, don't you care! Why aren't you doing something, we are about to perish! Wait a minute! Did they really think that Jesus, would have allowed his disciples to perish? I don't think so! We are talking about God's Son here. We are talking about those individuals who were doing what Jesus asked them to do. These were the followers of Jesus, obeying what Jesus had told them. But, he is in the same boat with them. Where is their faith?: Jesus asked.

No there was no chance of them perishing. Peter would later write in **II Peter 3:9** that Jesus was not slow in responding but purposefully waiting on men, not willing for anyone to perish. Maybe he was thinking about this very event.

I enjoy listening to the Brooklyn Tabernacle Choir sing and one of my favorites of their songs contains the line: *"In my moment of fear, through every doubt, every tear, there's a God whose been faithful to me."*

Later on In **John 16:33** Jesus told his disciples that they should expect trouble in this world because the world is full of trouble.

The encouraging part of his statement was that we are not alone in this world of trouble. Jesus said that he would not leave them comfortless and without hope, he would send the Comforter, the Helper to remain with them. The best news was that we don't have to overcome this troubled world, Jesus has already overcome this world of trouble and storm.

Though Jesus had not been crucified, buried and he had not risen from the grave in triumph yet, the victory was as good as done. It was as though it was already signed, sealed and delivered because of the sovereign Word of God. God's Will, will be done, on earth as it is in heaven.

Jesus, himself, had a moment of stress, a time where his heart was greatly troubled, and it was when he was in the garden praying to his he Father would say: *Nevertheless, not my will but Thine be done.* In his moment of great trouble, there was his Father hho would remain faithful to him.

Jesus did have a heavy heart and would sweat as though, that sweat were great drops of blood but even during all that he had no fear. There is no fear in God. So, neither do you need to fear.

So, stand still and hold his hand. *"Where is your faith?"*

Think about it. *Selah*

Day 63:
Practical Atheist?

"And without faith it is impossible to please Him, for whoever would draw near to God must believe that He exists and that He rewards those who seek Him."
Hebrews 11:6 ESV

Do you believe in God? Perhaps you don't and you call yourself an Atheist. Well, the truth is, God is not up for debate, neither does he need to be given credibility nor to be authorized by someone else. God is God and there is none beside him. Fact is fact and fact needs no adjustment, it just is. God is and it is the fool that has said in his heart, there is no God. **Psalm 53:1**

The Creator is not defined by the creation; as is written in **Romans 9:20 ESV** *"But who are you, O man, to answer back to God? Will what is molded say to its molder, 'Why have you made me like this?' Has the potter no right over the clay, to make out of the same lump one vessel for honorable use and another for dishonorable use?"*

We must come to the realization that we, the creation, can in no way think like or hope to understand the mind of the Creator.

A. W. Tozer puts it this way: *The creature thinks and speaks with creature thought and tries to understand the Creator."* It just cannot be done, it is humanly or creaturely impossible. The difficulty that the atheist has is that he or she cannot see and does not have the faith necessary to accept the reality of God.

Paul describes another aspect of belief in God, this is the **practical atheist**. *"They profess to know God, but they deny Him by their works. They are detestable, disobedient, unfit for any good work."* **Titus 1:16**

You say you believe in God but don't obey God? I wonder how this happens. One reason, perhaps, is because of the position and the power that those people have gained in life. Perhaps it's because they have been so blessed by God in many great ways, and they don't need to obey, they feel they are above other believers. Perhaps they have been teachers, pastors and evangelists and begin to proclaim the Word of God, but they are saying: Don't do what I do, do what I say.

What is coming through loud and clear is their true heart's desire. Their desire is not God desire. They say they know God but live as though they do not believe in God. They might as well not believe in God because they have become practical atheist. This is a dangerous and sad place to be.

Jesus tells a parable of a man who had two sons, he asked them to go out and work in the vineyard today. One said: You got to be kidding dad, it's just too hot out there, you have servants who will do that. After a while, the son thought about what he had done and went out into the field to work as his dad had asked him to do. The other son's reply to his dad was: Of course, father, I will go! But he didn't go. Which son was the one that was pleasing to his dad? The one who said no at first and then repented and obeyed. The other was a "practical atheist".

Be careful! Examine your life to make sure you are a practicing believer and a faithful servant of God not a "practical atheist"?

Think about it. *Selah*

Day 64:
That narrow, starlit strip

"The righteous pass away, the godly often pass away before their time. And no one seems to understand that God is protecting them from the evil to come. For the godly who die will rest in peace."
Isaiah 57:1 NKJV

My daughter Joni and her husband Heath are missionaries in Japan. A close friend of Joni and Heath, who were missionaries in Columbia South America and had three little children close to the ages of Joni and Heaths, died suddenly from cancer. It was very devastating to them.

This was the first death of a close friend who was of her age. Not only her age and a college friend but she, her husband and children were missionaries also but on the mission field in South America.

Particularly trying was the reality that Joni would not be able would not be able to attend her funeral. I shared something that William Jennings Bryan wrote upon a death of a believer friend of his: *"Christ has made of death a narrow, starlet strip between the companionship of yesterday, and the reunions of tomorrow."*

For the believer in Jesus, death is not an end, it is a pause. It is a pause between this temporary life and the beginning of eternal life. It is as though you have planned a great vacation, you have made all the reservations and planned all the things that you will do and everyone is packed and ready heading out but you cannot go right now because of responsibilities that you have, but when your work has ended, you will join them on that trip. There is a short time of sorrow but very soon you will be with them. They have just gone on ahead of you.

My dad often quoted that statement in funerals and added this statement that I believer was from Vance Havner: *"At the death of a believer, then tears will be gone, pain will be gone, for the former things will be passed away."* Referring to *Revelation* **21:14**

Isaiah wrote in **57:1** *"The righteous pass away, the godly often pass away, the godly often pass away before their time. And no one seems to understand that God is protecting them from the evil to come. For the godly who die will rest in peace."*

Memories are good, they strengthen our resolve to live for Christ and to encourage us to press all the more to finish the race and to reach the goal to obtain the reward of eternal life. Our memories can fade but eternity only grows brighter and clearer. So my friend, cling to the memories but reach for the goal.

Be comforted, as Paul wrote in **1 Thessalonians 4:18** be comforted with these words and comfort each other. His coming is upon us, he coming is nearer now that when we first believed. We haven't lost anyone, they have just finished first and are saving us a place in line.

Think about it. *Selah*

Day 65:
Which way?

"O people of Zion, who live in Jerusalem, you will weep no more. He will be gracious. If you ask for help. He will respond instantly to the sound of your cries. Though the Lord gave you adversity for food and affliction for drink, he will still be with you to teach you. You will see your teacher with your own eyes. And you will hear a voice say, 'This is the way: turn around and walk here.'" **Isaiah 30:19 - 21 NLT**

Remember the commercial that asked the question: *"What will you do, what you will do?"* Just that I remember it, means that it did the job it was created to do.

There are many times in our lives when we ask ourselves that question: What will I do now? We need knowledge and we need the wisdom to use the knowledge that we might have. We can only make decision based upon the knowledge that we have. It is when there is a void of knowledge or an ignorance of data that we are prevented from making confident decisions and living life in confidence.

We can always guess and make choices by chance but that will leave you in fear. I might be right or I might be wrong, that is trial and error. Just because something seems to be right or everybody else is doing it, does not make it right.

In **Proverbs 16:25** Solomon writes: *"There is a way that seems right but the end thereof leads to destruction."*

There is a sure way though and that is God's way which leads us in the way of truth and true knowledge. Jesus tells us that He is the way the truth and the life in **John 14:6** and in **James 1:5** we are told that God wants to guide us and to give us direction in any decision. In **John 16:13** Jesus gives the believer comfort by telling us that He would give us the Holy Spirit as a teacher, comforter and Help. In **Jeremiah 6:16** we are told that God's direction brings us peace of mind. In **Matthew 1:20** we discover God guiding Joseph and Mary to understand something beyond human understanding. We read in **Matthew 2:12** that even the Wise men needed direction and help in the way that they should take. Pharaoh, a pagan worshiper, was led to choose Joseph as a co-ruler in **Genesis 41:39 & 40.**

We read of many other non-believers in scripture whom God gave direction and used like Cyrus, to bring Israel home.

Joseph was pondering or wondering what he should do with Mary and then God showed up! Fear not! This is the way, walk ye in it.

Think about it. *Selah*

Day 66:
For unto you is born this day a Savior

"For unto you is born this day a Savior, who is Christ the Lord." **Luke 2:11 ESV**

Do you remember who were the one's who witness the coming of the Savior to earth?
Who was there to celebrate?

There were not a team of doctors and nurses for sure on that day that Jesus was born in Bethlehem. Probably just the animals in the stable actually witnessed the birth with Mary and Joseph that day. But there were others around, there were the shepherds, who came later that night. They came by personal invitation a heavenly invitation and no one else received one, just them. They were the only ones that were there that night; Mary, Joseph, the animals, the shepherds but all of heaven rejoiced. It was just the way the Father wanted it, of lowly birth.

How many shepherds were there? Well, the Bible uses the world shepherds so there more than one but most likely three. What I'm saying is that the number was small. The wise men came a couple years later, I can imagine that it takes quite a while following a star. The group of wise men were small in number as well.

Jesus didn't come with earthly pageantry. But there was a heavenly host that was the main crowd because this was a God thing. It was the heavenly host that handed out the invitation to the shepherds.

Jesus was the Good Shepherd who would care for His own sheep.

Think of it, the Creator of the world, this lost world came in truly lowly birth. How much lower could it be than in a stable?
But this was not a surprise to God, He was not disappointed, this was His plan. This earth is not His Kingdom anyway. But heaven was there in great number and with great celebration because this was the day! This was the day that God had been telling the world about for years, and now it has come!

This day was perfectly choreographed by God Almighty. It was perfect! It was His design. This was a God thing, it was His thing!

Mankind was born in sin and Jesus was born for our sin. He was to be that perfect sacrifice, the perfect atonement for the sin of the world.

Yes, it was a lowly birth but a glorious one as well. So, the angels "said" or I prefer to say, "sang": "GLORY TO GOD IN THE HIGHEST AND ON EARTH GOOD WILL TOWARD MEN!"

And it was a Merry Christmas joy and peace did come to earth on that night!

Think about it. *Selah*

Day 67:
Too little and too insignificant

"Therefore, my beloved, as you have always obeyed, so now, not only as in my presence but much more in my absence, work out your own salvation with fear and trembling, for it is God who works in you, both to will and to work for His good pleasure."
Philippians 2:13 & 13

Most likely you have said or at least you have heard someone say at one time or another: *"If that person would get saved, he or she could make a great impact for the cause of Christ."* ? We seem to think that it takes a popular, famous or well renowned person to be successful in the cause of Christ.

The truth is, Jesus is the one who supplies the power. Paul writes: *"It is God who works in you, both to will and to work for His good pleasure."* **Philippians 3:13 ESV** You can't be too little for God to use you but you could be too big for God to use you. He uses humble people, weak people and obscure people. If you think God could never use you, then you are the very person God is looking for.

If you will listen to God, and obey his leading in your life, then God will supply all the power, knowledge and financing to do that which He has called you to do.

You can't be too little, you can't be too insignificant, you cannot be overlooked for He is looking right at you.

Think about it. *Selah*

Day 68:
For such a time as this.

". . . Do not think to yourself that in the king's palace you will escape any more than all the other Jews. For if you keep silent at this time, relief and deliverance will rise for the Jews from another place, but you and your father's house will perish and who knows whether you have not come to the kingdom for such a time as this?"
Esther 4:13 & 14 ESV

This is the time! Don't tell God to wait, because you are not ready like those recorded in **Luke 9:57 - 62** and say I will follow you but first . . . . Sometimes God calls and there appears to be a conflict or at least a completing obligation. Remember, God already know all about you and your situation and obligations, so when He calls the correct response is yes, Lord, I will go. He is the provider not you. He is the supplier not you. He is the One who meets all our need to do what He asks of us.

Timing is the crucial thing with God. If you are not willing for God to use you, then he will use someone else, you cannot delay or wait, for now is the time. Who knows what will happen to us if we wait? There is no rerun in the call of God and that opportunity that he has placed before you will not come again. 'Timing' rather than time is of the essence.

Who knows but that God has placed you in this very situation for such a time as this? The offer is yours for the taking. Just do it.
Think about it. *Selah*

Day 69:
To feel the power and love of God

"But you will receive power when the Holy Spirit has come upon you, and you will be my witnesses in Jerusalem and in all Judea and Samaria, and to the end of the earth."
Acts 1:8 ESV

Written on the fly leaf of one of my Dad's preaching Bibles were these words:
"I want to feel the power, and love of God so in my life that I can look on a lost world as Jesus looked on it, and weep for their souls, beg for their souls, give my whole being to win their souls to God." With this writing my Dad, Glenn Elmore Thomas, a loving pastor and great man of God, expressed what was in his heart's desire.

William Murphy captured that same passion in his worship song: <u>One Pure And Holy Passion:</u>
    Give me a pure and holy passion,
    give me one magnificent obsession,
    give me a glorious ambition for my life,
    to run and follow hard after you."

Those words of my Dad have inspired me to strive for the same vision. With these Words my dad passed on to me that same desire. Paul wrote to Timothy *"And what you have heard from me in the presence of many witnesses entrust to faithful men who will be able to teach others also."* **2 Timothy 2:2 ESV**

Jesus promised the believer that power in **Acts 1:8** and that power was the power of the Holy Spirit. Jesus also

commissioned His followers to: *"Remain in His love and when You obey Me you remain in My love . . . I command you to love each other in the same way that I love you . . I have appointed you to produce fruit that will last . . ."*
John 15:9 - 17 ESV

Is this your desire? Is this your passion? The field is actually ripe for harvesting now, all that is needed is laborers. Will you go? Will you pass on to your children a magnificent obsession to run and follow hard after Christ?

Think about it. *Selah*

Day 70:
There were three men

"One of the criminals hanging beside Him scoffed, 'So, you're the Messiah, are you? Prove it by saving yourself- and us, too, while you're at it!' But the other criminal protested, 'Don't you fear God even when you are dying? We deserve to die for our evil deeds, but this man hasn't done anything wrong.' Then he said, Jesus, remember me when you come into your Kingdom.' and Jesus replied, 'I assure you, today you will be with me in paradise.'" **Luke 23:39 - 43 NLT**

There were three crosses erected upon Mount Calvary, the place of the skull. There were three men attached to those crosses, two convicted thieves and the other was Jesus the Son of God.

The one thief died in his sin to spend eternity in hell because of his sins. The other thief died from his sins, apart from his deeds, to spend eternity in Paradise with Jesus in his Kingdom.

The one on the middle cross died for the sins of the world. Forgiveness was offered to all who would follow the example of the repentant thief.

The inscription written in Aramaic, Latin and Greek above the cross of Jesus read: "Jesus of Nazareth, The King of the Jews" It proclaimed to all Who he was: He was the Messiah, the Christ, the promised one the King.

The unrepentant thief on the cross scoffed at Jesus to prove that he was the Son of God by coming down off the cross and while he was at it save him too. It would have been easy for Jesus to come down from the cross and save himself but if he did he would not have saved others. It was not the nails that held him on the cross, it was my sins and yours that demanded that he stay there but it was his great and awesome love that kept him there.

The sad story here is that if the scoffing thief would have asked forgiveness, he would have spent the rest of that day and all eternity with Jesus along with the repentant thief.

That is still true today, each of us is given the opportunity to accept eternal life by repenting of our sin. Some do, most don't.

Which one are you?

Think about it. *Selah*

Day 71:
A blessing to the nations

" 'O Israel, come back to me,' says the Lord. 'If you will throw away your detestable idols and go astray no more, and if you will swear by my name alone, and begin to live Good, honest lives and uphold justice, then you will be blessing to the nations of the world, and all people will come and praise my name.' "
Jeremiah 4:1 & 2 NLT

God blesses the nations of the world by His people. This was done in the Old Testament time, the New Testament as it is today. Though the nations hate and do all that Satan commands them to do, still there remains an innate understanding of the one and only and true God.

I like the classic movie **Ben Hur**. One of my favorite lines from that movie is where the Pro Counsel Arrius said to Ben Hur after a naval battle: *"In His eagerness to save you, your God has saved the Roman Fleet."* Yes, God is eager to save the world by our carrying of His Good News to the nations. That is the Great Commission and the Great Commission Displays God's great eagerness to save the world.

God's eagerness is expressed in the verse that is perhaps the most well known and most quoted of all in the Bible: **John 3:16 - 17 ESV** *"For God so loved the world, that He gave His only Son, that whoever believes in Him should not perish but have eternal life. For God sent not His Son into the world, to condemn the world, but that the world might* *be saved through Him."* We also see his eager desire in **II Peter 3:9 ESV** *". . . not wishing that any should perish but that all should reach repentance."*

In **Acts 27** we read of Paul's shipwreck on his way to Rome. God had told Paul that he would spare those in the boat because of Paul: **Acts 27:23 ESV** *"For this very night there stood before me an angel of the God to whom I belong and whom I worship, and he said, 'Do not be afraid, paul; you must stand before Caesar. And behold, God hs granted you all those who sail with you. So take heart, men, for I have faith in God that it will be exactly as I have been told."* And they were saved because of Paul. In Ben Hur, it wasn't the fleet of ships, it was those in those ships that Jesus eagerly wanted to save. God saved them all and he want to save you also.

Think about it. *Selah*

Day 72:
I'm gonna' miss him.

"Casting all your anxieties upon Him because He cares for you." **I Peter 5:7 ESV**

My oldest son, Justin and his wife Kathy had to take their middle child Colman who was five year old at the time, to the emergency room after he fell on a fence post and received
a big cut in his hand. Their two year old son, Nash told his mother, Kath: *"Mom, I'm gonna' miss him."* I'm not sure if he thought Colman was going to stay at the hospital or just go on to heaven? But whatever, he was going to be missed.

I guess in his own way, Nash was saying: *"I care for Colman."* It's good to have people around you that care for you and it is very troubling when you don't have anyone who you know really care for you. They want to be around you when you are happy and they long to be with you when you hurt.

Jesus wants us to cast our care upon him, that means that he longs for us to bring our cares to him and leave them there. Leave them there because he wants them, he desires to sooth them and to solve them. All he asks of us is to trust him with them. To know that he will come to us with His loving arms and envelope us with them. He will pull us close to Him so we can hear His loving heart. So we can feel the great peace that comes with that act of trust.

His great love is expressed in his care for us and our soul. He isn't just concerned for the time being but for eternity. His care for us last forever. His care will never fail, and he will never leave us uncared for.

He is patient, kind, genuine, longsuffering, enduring, trustworthy, gracious, merciful and effective. When we don't come to him with those cares that we have, he misses us.

Think about it. *Selah*

Day 73:
Be still

"Be still, and know that I am God. I will be exalted among the nations, I will be exalted in the earth." **Psalm 46:10 ESV**

I don't like to be in a situation where I feel helpless, unapt or not able to bring about a solution to a problem. The truth is we all find ourselves in just that situation many times in our lives. There are many, many times when we find ourselves in need of help.

It has been in these situations that I have found that I have an asset that is more than able to meet those demands with unbelievable resolutions. I find that these weak moments are God moments. What I have found to be the answer is: Be still, be quiet and listen and discover added strength, greater power and perfect peace.

Here are some of those moments:

When I come up against a wall, I stand still and let God take over. **Psalm 18:29** *". . by my God I can leap over a wall. This God-his way is perfect."*

When I have done all I can do, I stand still and see my salvation right before my eyes, **Exodus 14:13**

When I have come to the end of my strength, I stand still because it is there God's strength begins. **2 Corinthians 12:10**

When I have felt unloved and unappreciated, I stand still, then Jesus reminds me I should expect trouble in the world but this trouble will not overcome me, He has overcome it. **John 16:33**

When I feel I can't do this anymore, I stand still to hear God tell me keep going, I'll finish this work with you. **Philippians 1:6**

When I feel all alone, I stand still and listen for the voice of Jesus who call me his friend.
John 15:15

"Be still and know that I am God." **Psalm 46:10**

Think about it. *Selah*

Day 74:
The Lord's Day

"I was in the Spirit on the Lord's day, and I hear behind me a loud voice like a trumpet saying, ' Write what you see in a book and send it to the seven churches..."
Revelation 1:10 & 11 ESV

King David wrote in **Psalm 122:1 ESV** *"I was glad when they said to me, 'Let us go to the house of the Lord!'"* I too can honestly say that as well. I am glad when Sunday comes. Israel met on the Sabbath Day which was Saturday. Today Christians meet on Sunday which we call The Lord's Day. We meet on Sunday because it was the day of Jesus' Resurrection.

The Apostle John mentions it in **Revelation 1:10** where he was in the Spirit on the Lord's Day. In **John 20:1** We read of the first day of the week. **Acts 20:7** Luke records that the believer's met together in the evening on the first day of the week when they were gathered together to break bread and listen to a sermon from Paul. Sunday has been the day of worship for the followers of Jesus.

I wonder, do you enjoy the Lord's house? The body of believers with whom you worship meet there to praise and worship together, to encourage each other and love each other, or at least they should. We are strengthened there, we listen and learn there. Jesus commanded us to be the icon of Him and that icon is love. They will know that we are Christians by our love. **John 13:35 ESV** *"By* *this all people will know that you are my disciples if you have love for one another."*

In today's church houses we see the cross and that reminds of what Jesus did for us and what we need to do to follow him. We must take up our cross daily and gladly bear it.

The believer worships with the singing of songs, hymns and spiritual song and we sing from the heart. When we go into the house of the Lord we sing praise to our God and worship His holy name. Worship brings peace and Joy to our soul. It is in praise that we experience God because He inhabits our praise.

When we go into the house of the Lord we listen to His Word being proclaimed. It is by our being still and knowing that The Lord is God. Worship brings peace to our soul, joy to our spirit even in the midst of our struggle. God's Word brings us knowledge, truth and wisdom to correct the many lies which surround us.

Are you ready for worship? A. W. Tozar has said: *"I can safely say, on the authority of all that is revealed in the Word of God, that any man or woman on this earth who is board and turned off by worship is not ready for heaven."*

Don't be bored, be glad!

Think about it. *Selah*

Day 75:
Hey! This world is rotten!

After this the Lord appointed seventy-two others and sent them on ahead of him, to by two, into every town and place where He himself was about to go. And He said to them, 'The harvest is plentiful, but the labors are few. Therefore pray earnestly to the Lord of the harvest to send out laborers into His field.' "
Luke 10:1 & 2 ESV

It's very obvious that this world is rotting away. Things aren't getting better in any stretch of the imagination. The question we should be asking is not *"Why hasn't the Lord done something."* The question for the believer is: *"Why haven't I done what God has asked of me today?"*

The reason the world is rotten is that the harvest is here and I am allowing it to rot in the field. As Jesus sent the seventy two out to every place and every town when he was on this earth, he is now sending us to go every place and every town with his Good News and make disciples.

Because we spend too much time looking at the bad things others are doing, we forget to obey the Lord of the harvest and do as He has commanded. I ask myself this question: *"Why, do we spend so much time and money in my church trying to meet it's needs when there are so many lost sheep out "there" beyond the walls of the church."*

Albert Eisenstein has said: *"We live in a dangerous world not because of the wicked people on it but because of the good people who do nothing about it."*

I'm thinking that the need we have in the church is not better equipment, programs and ideas, the need is for it members to become obedient labors in the field. The harvest is plentiful and the crop will rot if we do not harvest it. Are we obeying the Lord of the harvest?

'The harvest is plentiful, but the labors are few. Therefore pray earnestly to he Lord of the harvest to send out laborers into His field.'

Think about it. *Selah*

Day 76:
Where is heaven and who is in it?

"Then I saw a new heaven and a new earth, for the first heaven and the first earth had passed away and the sea was no more. And I saw the holy city Jerusalem coming down out of heaven from God, prepared as a bride adorned for her husband. And I heard a loud voice from the throne saying, 'Behold, the dwelling place of God is with man. He will dwell with them, and they will be his people. And God himself will be with them as their God. He will wipe away every tear from their eyes, and heath shall be no more, neither shall there be mourning, nor crying, nor pain anymore, for the former things have passed away. And he who was seated on the throne said, 'Behold, I am making all things new.' Also he said, 'Write this down, for these words are trustworthy and true. And he said to me, 'It is done! I am the Alpha and the Omega, eh beginning and the end. To the thirsty I will give from the spring of the water of life without payment. To the one who conquers will have this heritage, and I will be his God and he will be my son."
Revelation 21:1 - 6 ESV

Heaven! The most pleasing destination that can be conceived in the mind of anyone. It is the place most people want to be able to go. Where is it? Who is in it? What does Jesus and His Word say about Heaven?

He tells us children will be there. **Mark 10:14**

He tells us it is His Kingdom and He has gone to prepare it for us, the believer. **John 14:1 - 3**

He tells us that it's citizens will have newly created bodies and have eternal life. **2 Corinthians 5:17**

He tells us it is not on this earth, this earth will pass away. **Revelation 21:1**

He tells us all things will be new there. **Revelation 21:5**

He tells us that the poor in spirit or those who have realized their need for Jesus, will be there. **Matthew 5:3**

He tells us the forgiven will be there. **Matthew 25:21**

The persecuted will be there. **Hebrews 11**

He tells us that those who died in the Lord will be there. **1 Thessalonians 5:16 & 17, Revelation 14:3**

He tells us Satan and his angels won't be there. **Revelation 20:10**

He tells us the fearful, unbelieving and the like won't be there. **Revelation 21:8**

The big question is, are you going to be there?
"Behold now is the favorable time; behold now is the day of salvation."
2 Corinthians 6:2 *ESV*

Think about it. *Selah*

Day 77:
Count it all loss

"But whatever gain I had, I counted as loss for the sake of Christ. Indeed, I count everything as loss because of the surpassing worth of knowing Christ Jesus my Lord. For his sake I have suffered the loss of all things and count them as rubbish, in order that I may gain Christ." **Philippians 3:7 & 8 ESV**

To follow Christ, to give him my all, is to forfeit everything, to give it up for the cause of Christ. If you follow Christ you will find yourself in a place that is far beyond you. You will find yourself in a situation well beyond your own mind to comprehend, you will find yourself beyond where your wildest dreams can take you. If you follow Christ you will find yourself in situations where you are incapable of being naturally. You wonder how you got there.

When you are following Christ, having given all you have to give, you find yourself in the grip of faith. You have come to the place where you know for certain that, if God does not step in, then you are destined for failure. This is exactly where faith brings you, in the hand of Christ.

God takes you to where you are because he wants you to see he is a good Father, and his Son is faithful and good as well. He wants you to know and experience the good and helpful Holy Spirit who is a powerful and capable teacher, a very present comfort and help in doing what

He is leading you to do.

God is our hope, he is our supply. So go with him and see great things that only can be done through him.

Think about it. *Selah*

Day 78:
Wow! What a wicked world!

"When the captain for the Roman soldiers handling the executions saw what had happened, he praised God and said, Surely this man was innocent.'"
Luke 23:47 NLT

If you listen much to the news or the talk around town, you are sure to hear the talk about how wicked this world is. And this world is filled with wickedness of all sorts. We can find people who are quick to prey upon children, the disadvantaged, the weak, the little and the helpless.

Yet, in spite of all this wickedness, in the very bastions of this wicked world, I marvel at this thought: *"Why are there so many good people in a world that is full of wickedness?"* How does that happen?

In the very midst of the crucifixion of Jesus, we see the captain of the Roman guards, who had the responsibility of carrying out crucifixions for the government, realizing and acknowledging to those present, that the person who was the recipient of this public display of wrath, was the very Son of God. In the middle of it all, there was the realization of good.

The marvel to me is not that the world is so wicked but that how many good people can be found in the middle of all this wickedness? What are they doing there? They are there because they do not think that anything can be done about it.

This brings me to another shocking thought: "These good people that we find in the darkness of this world, may not and most likely are not believers and followers of our Lord Jesus Christ!" If they are not, they cannot go to heaven! Does that bother you? It bothers me. And this is the very reason that Jesus has given us the mission of telling others about the Good News and making disciples, they do not know about it or understand it and it's the Good News to them, it's The Great Commission.

I like what I have heard Ravi Zacharias say: *"Jesus didn't come into the world to make bad people good, He came into this world to make dead people alive!"*

Jesus said it this way to Nicodemus: *"For God so loved the world that he gave his only begotten Son, that whosoever believers in him should not perish (die) but have eternal "life".* **John 3:16 Nicodemus** didn't understand it and neither do the others of this world.

Is our world wicked? Yes. The world needs to be rescued and we have been sent with the cure. They can see the cure but they do not know how to apply the cure. Nature itself, clearly displays the goodness of God, yet they refuse to acknowledge him. Just like the Captain of the Roman soldiers at the crucifixion of Jesus, *"Yes, Surely He was God!"* All those around the cross mocked Jesus but it was clear that he was the Son of God.

I guess the awesome thought here is, what manner of love is it that would compel God to display his great love to such a wicked world by sending his Son to die for them so that they might live and not die?

"The Lord is not slow to fulfill his promise as some count slowness, but is patient toward you, not wishing that any should perish, but that all should reach repentance."
2 Peter 3:9 ESV

God is waiting on us to go. So, our job is to tell these good people of God's Good News. Find them and tell them! Think about it. *Selah*

Day 79: Go ye therefore!

"And Jesus came and said to them. All authority in heaven and on earth has been given to me. Go therefore and make disciples of all nations, baptizing them in the name of the Father and of the Son and of the Holy Spirit, teaching them to observe all that I have commanded you. And behold, I am with you always, to the end of the age."
Matthew 28:19 & 20

To go is the call of Jesus to us. We often refer to this commandment as the Great Commission. Go and make disciples is what Jesus said that His followers were to do. For some reason, this seems very difficult and at least a struggle for the church to answer this call of Jesus today.

Lottie Moon often would write back to the Southern Baptist Churches in America to send more men. But the call fell on deaf ears. Not many would go.

It is not only the churches and people who struggle with this but the Mission Boards have that same struggle as they try to decide what to do and what not to do. The call is clear, the need is great, the fields are still white and the laborers are still few.

We are seeing rotten things happen in the world and perhaps it is because the fields have gone un-harvested and now they are beginning to rot. I often wonder why the labors are few? There are few laborers and great fear and certainly little joy in serving Christ.

Have you ever noticed the life of those who share the Gospel with others? There is a great joy there. There is an obvious spirit of confidence and no fear at all.

These people are engaged in telling others about what Christ has done for them. They joy in contagious.

Here is the truth that is found here. There is a joy in serving Jesus! The happiest time in the life of a believer is when he is telling another person about what Jesus has done in his life.

May I present this challenge to you? The truth is that the only way you will ever begin to share Jesus with others is that you need to make an intentional effort to begin. After you intentionally do it one time, it's a little easier the next time. As you continue to share it will not be long before it will become natural for you to share and before you know it, sharing is instinctive, it is just part of you.

Until you intentionally begin and make plans to share, it will never happen.

Think about it. *Selah*

**Day 80:
Random Acts of Kindness**

"Don't you realize how kind, tolerant, and patient God is with you? Or don't you care? Can't you see how kind he has been in giving you time to turn from your sin?"
Romans 2:4 NLT

God is good and kind and the expression of His goodness and kindness is shown in His great patience toward us. *"The goodness of God leads you to repentance?"* **KJV** It is His "seemingly slowness" to judge us, that is actually is intentionally longsuffering to us. He is patient with us and that gives us time to realize just how good, gracious and merciful He actually is. **2 Peter 3:9 God** can act quickly but He chooses to be kind and wait.

Kindness causes people to stop and take another look. Kindness is the mirror that God uses to force those who cannot see His great face or feel His loving heart, to experience them. Kindness is a tool that we can use to make and to force, even the most hardened individual, to stop and see God.

Do you find it difficult to share your faith with others? I think most Christians would say yes here. There is a very simple but daring way to share what God has done for us with others. It's quick, it's simple yet it leaves a most effective impact.

We have just read that the kindness of God leads to repentance, haven't we? So, let's use this method of random acts of kindness. All that it takes is to be observant. If you notice someone at a restaurant that seems to you might be in need, pay for someone's meal and leave a note: "God has been good to me and I think He wants me to do this for you. God loves you." **John 3:16** *"For God so loved the world that He gave...."* Don't thank me, thank God. Then leave, don't sign your name, don't do anything else. That is power!

It could be many things: Cutting someone's grass, painting a door, fixing a broken toy, giving a smile. It could be just saying: "I'm going to pray for my meal right now and I wonder if there is something I could pray for you?" When you leave them, leave a note. Just be observant.

"Or do you not know that the kindness of God leads you to repentance?"

Think about it. *Selah*

Day 81:
Is something bothering you?

"Don't fret or worry, Instead of worrying, pray. Let petitions and praises shape your worries into prayers." **Philippians 4:6 Message**

Are you worried? Are you at the point where you just don't know what to do? Well my friend, may I suggest something that is easy to say but, although small, not easy to put into action? FORGET ABOUT IT!!!! STOP!!!! Just pray about it, give it to God and then leave it with Him. Look up. Jesus said as He was sharing with his disciples about some things that would happen in the last days. We can apply those words to our situation now: *"When these things begin to happen, look up, lift up your heads, for your redemption draws nigh."* **Luke 21:28**

Paul writes: *"Don't fret or worry. Instead of worrying, pray. Let petitions and praises shape your worries into prayers, letting God know your concerns. Before you know it, a since of God's wholeness, everything coming together for good, will come and settle you down. It's wonderful what happens when Christ displaces worry at the center of your life."* **Philippians 4:6 & 7 Message**

Hey! Paul was in prison when he wrote these words. Henry Blackaby comments in <u>Experiencing God Day by Day</u>: *He* (Paul) *lived in a corrupt nation, worldly values were in vogue, he was falsely accused, depreciated from his friends and family, his motives were questioned by other Christians, some we're trying to undermine all that he had done in the churches he had established, he was sick and facing the possibility of execution."* Now, in the grip of all that, Paul writes: *"Quit worrying brothers and sisters!"*

How could he say that? He could say that because, despite all that man had done to him in the past, doing to him right now and might do to him in the future, he knew that if God was for him, what could man do to him? **Romans 8:31** He did not fear those who could kill the body, but He feared Him Who was able to destroy the soul. **Luke 12:5**

So from prison, Paul concludes with these encouraging words:

"Summing it all up, friends, I'd say you'll do best by filling your minds and meditating on things true, noble, reputable, authentic, compelling, gracious-the best, not the worst; the beautiful, not the ugly; things to praise, not things to curse. Put into practice what you learned from me, what you heard and saw and realized. Do that, and God, who makes everything work together, will work you into his most excellent harmonies."
Philippians 4: 8 & 9 Message

So, I say from my comfortable home and at my convenient computer: Look up, fix your eyes on Christ, your Redeemer, He who weaves all thing to together for your good.
FORGET ABOUT IT!!!! STOP IT!!!

Think about it. *Selah*

Day 82:
Know what you believe

"Dear Theophilus, in the first volume of this book (The Gospel of Luke) I wrote on everything that Jesus began to do and teach until the day he said good-bye to the apostles, the ones he had chosen through the Holy Spirit. and was taken up to heaven. After this death, he presented himself alive to them in many different settings over a period of forty days. In face-to-face meetings, he talked to them about things concerning the kingdom of God. As they met and ate meals together, he told them that they were on no account to leave Jerusalem but 'must wait for what the Father promised: the promise you heard from me. John baptized in water; you will be baptized in the holy Spirit. And soon.' "Acts **1:1 - 5 Message**

Doctor Luke knew the importance of the new believer, the Christian, to know what he believes. Theophilus was a close friend and perhaps new believer, who needed to know the truth and so Luke began to give him a clear account of what Jesus was all about.

What we call <u>The Gospel of Luke</u> was the first letter that Luke wrote to Theophilus and the book we have designated <u>The Acts of the Apostles</u> was the second letter. Like Theophilus, the believers today need to know the truth. The early Church Fathers also knew the importance of having a clear understand of Biblical Truth. Scripture had to be hand written and there were few copies of Scripture available, so they would have the people learn, memorize and recite together various sanctioned or approved creeds that simply laid out the basic true doctrine of the faith.

The Anthansian Creed is one of those creeds, it was detailed and lengthy. I like the way it describes the trinity with these words:

"The Father is made of none, neither created nor begotten. The Son is of the Father alone, not made, nor created but begotten. The Holy Spirit is of the Father and the Son: not made nor created, nor begotten, but proceeding (Issuing). *God exists in himself and of himself. His being he owes to no one. His substance is indivisible. He had no part but is single in his unitary being."*

A. W. Tozer would use this creed to relate God and man. God is the Creator and man is the creature, and the work of the Creator. The creature cannot understand the Creator because he only has a creature mind with only creature thoughts. The mind of the Creator is far beyond the ability of the creature to understand therefore he must, by faith, trust and rely on and in the Creator.

Our best understanding though, comes from asking the Creator and trusting he who proceeds from the Father, The Holy Spirit, to give us the faith to believe and added understanding.

"For what can be known about God is plain to them, because God has shown it to them. For his invisible attributes, namely, his eternal power and divine nature, have been clearly perceived, ever since the creation of the world, in the things that have been made." **Romans 1:19 & 20 ESV**

Think about it. *Selah*

Day 83:
Contented

"Not that I speak in regard to need, for I have learned in whatever state I am, to be content." **Philippians 4:11**

What does your prayer life look like? When you think of praying to God, what is it that has compelled you to bow your head and pray? Is it that you have been prompted by the many blessings that God has given you; your family, your health, your job, your friends, your provision and they like? Maybe many of them contain your praises to God for His gift of salvation, or your church and the body of believers that encourage you. Do they glorify God for all He has done?

I'm sure those things are there from time to time but most of the time, and more often than not, they contain things that you have asked God for such as help or supply of a great need. Well, Jesus told his disciples to do just that and he encouraged them to come boldly with requests. But, are those requests that you have been asking of God, are they actual needs that you have?

Paul, says that he has "learned" to be content with what he has. He says that the situations of life that come and go, are just that, things that come and go. They are things that are temporary events and he has learned to be OK with them. He is saying they aren't real needs that he would regard as real needs.

Perhaps Paul was remembering the three times that he had asked God to remove a thorn in his life, that he felt was a great need, and God answered his prayer with these words: *"My grace is sufficient."* **2 Corinthians 12:9 Paul** discovered that the thorn was an attribute in which he could boast.

What is your need? God wants to meet that need. He wants you to ask boldly but most of all He wants you to be content with His leading and answers. He wants you to trust Him and to know that He is with you and will never leave you and that He will with the difficulty that is before you, make you a glorious example of God's grace.

I like what Anne Graham Lots says in her book *Why?*: *"The secret to contentment is to be totally yielded to God. To climb up onto the lap of your heavenly Father by faith, let Him wrap His arms of love around you, and then just nestle down into His will."*

That is a good definition of prayer, talking and being content, *"... just nestle down into His will."*

Think about it. *Selah*

Day 84:
Eternal vigilance

"Therefore, my beloved brothers, be steadfast, immovable, always abounding in the work of the Lord, knowing that in the Lord your labor is not in vain."
1Chorinthians 15:58 ESV

It was President Ronald Reagan who said: *"Eternal vigilance is the price of freedom."* Never give up, press on, reach for the mark of the prize; let us be determined to do that which Jesus has called us to do. Never give in, never give up!

John Philpot Curran, an Irish politician, lawyer and judge said: *"The condition upon which God hath given liberty to man is eternal vigilance."*

Paul the Apostle encouraged the believer to be steadfast, immovable, always abounding in the work. That is how we are to react to things in life. Be vigilant, be resilient, be persistent, and always be dependent upon Jesus as our source of strength.

Think about yourself for a moment: are you where you should be in your Christian life? Have you slowed down or stopped serving Christ as you did in the past? If so, what is it that has hindered you in the work? What is it that has slowed you down? Paul asks this question to the believers at the church of Galatia. **Galatians 5:7 The** question is one that perhaps we should ask ourselves from time to time: "What is it that is hindering us in doing what we feel Jesus would have us do?"

Let us be vigilant in the work, strive to be resilient to the hindrances in life and never, ever, give up!
Think about it. *Selah*

Day 85:
Like what you do

"Whatever we do, it is because Christ's love controls us. Since we believe that Christ died for everyone, we also believe that we have all died to the old life we used to live."
2 Corinthians 5:14 NLT

King George V wrote the fly leaf of the Bible of a friend, *"The secret of happiness is not to do what you like to do, but to like what you have to do."*

They say that if you love your work, you will never work a day in your life. The same is true with happiness: if you determine to like what you have to do you will always be happy. Be happy doing what is necessary to do.

The believer has a glorious ambition and that is to please Jesus, to be diligent in our work for him so that we might hear from him at the end of our life on earth: *"Well done my child, you fought the fight with diligence, you ran the race with persistence and you finished the work. You were happy serving me, so, enter into the place that I have prepared just for you."*

The love of Christ controls us and it constrains us to keep on keeping on. I am most content, happy and love doing what God has given me to do! Don't you? I am happiest when I am sharing with others what Jesus has done for me. I think I'll tell someone right now!

Think about it. *Selah*

Day 86:
A Bully

"But you must be careful with this freedom of yours. Do not cause a brother or sister with a weaker conscience to stumble. . . . So because of your superior knowledge, a weak Christian, for whom Christ died, will be destroyed. And you are sinning against Christ when you sin against other Christians by encouraging them to do something they believe is wrong." **1 Corinthians 8:9 - 12 NLT**

No one likes a bully. A bully is someone who pushes himself or herself over another person who is perceived to be weaker, or who will not push back. A bully is actually a very insecure person, a bully is one who is not able to accomplish things by his or her own merit and may feel there is nothing desirable about himself other than the ability to strong arm another person.

We find bullies everywhere in life, at every age and even in the church. We find those who are wise in their own eyes and are intent on destroying other believers, even new believers by pushing their mind-set on them and label those who do not hold their opinion as too liberal or too conservative. They measure others by the measuring stick of their little group and are perfectly content, and even feel impassioned to destroy another believer just because they do not measure up.

Here is an example of bullying that is found in most every church, they are worship bullies. What is a worship bully?

This is a group of people in the church who make it their aim to bully anyone who does not share the same preference or comfort zone of worship style.

Let me take a brief survey. Does your church have a group that make light of those who prefer hymn in worship? What about the group who ridicule those who prefer contemporary praise and worship music, do you find those in your church? What about a group who enjoy measuring a person's spirituality by the choice of music they may even question the credibility of those who lead worship by what they ware? What about you, are you bothered by tennis shoes and un-tucked shirts? If a pastor reads his sermons or prayer, are there those who consider it boring? What about a pastor who loud and use a lot of humor in their sermons, does that turn them off? Does worship require specific instruments and accompaniment? I could go on and on but the point is, all these things are worship bullies. Don't be a bully, be a worshiper. Focus on Jesus don't be a stumbling block.

A. W. Tozer has written: *"I can safely say, on the authority of all that is revealed in the Word of God, that any man or woman on this earth who is bored and turned off by worship is not ready for heaven."*

"But you must be careful with this freedom of yours. Do not cause a brother or sister with a weaker conscience to stumble." **1 Corinthians 8:9 NLT**

Think about it. *Selah*

Day 87:
You're pleasing to God when you rejoice and sing

"I will sing to the Lord as long as I live; I will sing praise to my God while I have being. May my meditation be pleasing to him, for I rejoice in the Lord."
Psalm 104:33 - 34 ESV

There is great joy in praising God, singing to God and thinking about God. If you ever feel down, just start praising God and you find him, he inhabits praise that is where he lives. You don't even have to have a pleasant voice to sing to God, because it is pleasing to him and that is all that matters. It is he that has made us after all and that also means your specific voice. It may not be pleasing to other people but you aren't singing to them anyway. When you sing, it pleases him! Your singing brings out a big smile on his face.

Meditating on God just naturally brings out laughter, joy and singing. Thinking about God just makes you want to rejoice. Paul said in **Philippians 4:4** *"Rejoice in the Lord always, again I say, Rejoice!"* I like to say it way: Hey, fellow believer, rejoice in the Lord at all times, especially when things don't seem to be going your way because it is going God's way, so let me say it again . . . REJOICE!

        Praise God
        Sing to God
        Think about God
        Thank God
        Look for opportunities to tell others about what God has done.

God's way is the best way and it is the way of rejoicing. People need to know about it and they will when you rejoice.

"I will sing to the Lord as long as I live; I will sing praise to my God while I have being." **Psalm 104:33 ESV**

Think about it. *Selah*

Day 88:
Is anything happening?

"All authority in heaven and on earth has been given to me. Go therefore and make disciples . . . ." **Matthew 28:19 & 20 ESV**

Have you been praying passionately about something you are experiencing right now and yet you feel God has not addressed your prayer? You feel you have been and are faithful but where is God?

Did you know that if you are obedient to do God's will, it doesn't mean that you won't have difficulties? We are to make disciples but there will be struggles in the going. **Matthew 28:19 & 20**

Jesus said that we are in the world but not of this world, and the reason we are still in this world is to bring him glory and to give him glory by doing His will. When he called us he go, he already knew about the thing we would experience and he already made the provisions available for meeting them.

When He meets our need He receives glory. If your prayer has not been met yet, perhaps God is using you to meet the need of someone else's prayer right now. He hasn't forgotten you or your need. Sometimes we just don't understand because of our limited vision or knowledge.

Remember when Jesus was told about Lazarus and he said: *"This illness does not lead to death. It is for the glory of God, so that the Son of God may be glorified through it."* **John 11:4 ESV Something** big was about to happen, but only Jesus knew about it at the time. Maybe Jesus is encouraging a weaker believer with your faithfulness, your patience and your steadfastness in time of suffering. It could be that someone is watching you right now in the midst of your difficulty and is getting strength by it. Remember God is not bound by time but is all about timing. In the fullness of time God sent his Son.

Be patient, keep listening, keep working and see God's almighty hand.

Think about it. *Selah*

Day 89:
Commit To Faithful Men

"And what you have heard from me in the presence of many witnesses entrust to faithful men who will be able to teach others also." **2 Timothy 2:2 ESV**

Faithful men attract faithful men. All people admire the faithful, the committed and the steadfast. Faithfulness is the chief quality that companies are seek in filling positions of responsibility. Faithfulness is what make for good leaders. Paul tells Timothy that he needs to find faithful followers who would be as committed to him as Timothy was to Paul. Timothy was a faithful protégé of the Apostle Paul.

John Wooden was a talented basketball coach and he was able to inspire and impassion many young men as well. Some of the qualities that he passed on to his players were these:

"Talent is God given. Be humble
Fame is man given. Be grateful.
Conceit self-given. Be careful.

If you're not making mistakes, you're not doing anything.
I'm certain a doer makes mistakes

Be true to yourself, help others.
Make each day your masterpiece.
Make friendships a fine art.
Give thanks for your blessings and pray for guidance
Drink deeply from good books especially the Bible"

Life does not have a dress rehearsal nor is there an act 2. Make the most of your days and you will know happiness and joy in life. Be faithful and true in all you do and in everything that you do, do all for the glory of God.

Don't go through life alone commit what you have learned to other faithful friends.

Think about it. *Selah*

Day 90:
Life verses

"But life is worth nothing unless I use it for doing the work assigned me by The Lord Jesus, The work of telling to others the Good News of God's mighty kindness and love."
Acts 20:24 Living Bible

As I sought God's will in my life and as He led me through the various phases of my life, I had a verse that served as a definition and a guide that I found descriptive of God's moving in my life. I found that as I went through life my focus and needs would change as I grew. As my focus and needs changed so did my life verse change.

As a young person starting out my great need was confidence and guidance for every day and the verse that was descriptive of that time in life was **Proverbs 3:5 & 6 NKJV** *"Trust in the Lord with all your heart and lean not to thy own understanding. In all your ways acknowledge him and he shall direct you path."* And I found him faithful every day. He was there guiding me, leading me and giving me more and more confidence. God placed specific people in my life that would meet that need. It was his voice behind me saying: *"This is the way walk ye in it."* **Jeremiah 6:16 ESV** In his way I found peace and safety.

As I begin to gain confidence, experience and knowledge my goal was to be genuine, real and true to God's Word. I didn't want to be like everyone else, I wanted to be the man God wanted me to be. There seemed to be many new ideas and methods that were frequently competing for my attention and biding consideration. The verse that seemed to speak to me at that time was:. **2 Corinthians 4:1 & 2** *"It is God himself, in his mercy, who has given us this wonderful work (of telling his Good News to others) and so we never give up. We do not try to trick people into believing - we are not interested in fooling anyone. We never try to get anyone to believe that the Bible teaches what it doesn't. All such shameful methods we forgo. We stand in the presence of God as we speak and so we tell the truth, as all who know us will agree."* **Living Bible**

Retirement has now come and I have taken a step back and allowing others to step to the forefront. I have been comforted to still see the hand of God in my life, still there, still guiding and he has given me a desire to share those insights and observations to other faithful men and women. My verse now is **Acts 20:24** *"But life is worth nothing unless I use it for doing the work assigned me by The Lord Jesus, The work of telling to others the Good News of God's mighty kindness and love."* **Living Bible**

Did you notice, life did change and the needs in life changed as well but the assignment remains the same: Go and make disciples! The message is still the same.

Think about it. *Selah*

www.ingramcontent.com/pod-product-compliance
Lightning Source LLC
Chambersburg PA
CBHW071453040426
42444CB00008B/1317